After a difficult youth of violence and petty crime, Bill attended a theological college at the age of twenty-one. At twenty-three he started working as the manager of a drop-in and alcoholic rehabilitation centre in Melbourne, and subsequently became the youngest-ever superintendent of the Ballarat City Mission in its history of more than a century. He has dedicated his life and career to helping and inspiring disadvantaged people to realise their own potential, working with prisoners and those with special needs for many years. In his fifties, Bill completed a Bachelor of Arts at Deakin University, the first of many qualifications, including as a life coach. For much of his life he has been an ultramarathon runner, and has competed with the world's best Yiannis Kouros and folk hero Cliffy Young a number of times in the famous Colac Six-Day Race. The enormous resilience he has displayed in his running and throughout his life has been an inspiration and a model for others.

Driven

When you realise someone else thinks you
have potential, you'll start believing it yourself

BILL SUTCLIFFE

ALLEN&UNWIN
SYDNEY • MELBOURNE • AUCKLAND • LONDON

This edition published in 2023
First published in 2023

Allen & Unwin
Cammeraygal Country
83 Alexander Street
Crows Nest NSW 2065
Australia
Phone: (61 2) 8425 0100
Email: info@allenandunwin.com
Web: www.allenandunwin.com

*Allen & Unwin acknowledges the Traditional Owners of the Country on which we
live and work. We pay our respects to all Aboriginal and Torres Strait Islander
Elders, past and present.*

 A catalogue record for this
book is available from the
National Library of Australia

ISBN 978 1 76011 332 2

Set in 12.6/18.2 pt Bembo Std by Midland Typesetters, Australia
Printed and bound in Australia by the Opus Group

10 9 8 7 6 5 4 3 2 1

This book is dedicated to my wife of fifty-five years, Bev.
When just a teenager she pointed me in the right direction
And since then has not only walked with me on an incredible journey
But has been a major part of it.

Contents

Content note:

This book deals with the physical and sexual
abuse of a minor and suicidal ideation.

Foreword

Bill Sutcliffe is a very special person who has come through life with exceptional success. He is to be greatly admired, and his storytelling skills are second to none. *Driven* follows his journey from a lad growing up in a tough and dangerous environment, to his sporting achievements, to his work on farms and then in City Missions and prisons, and as a life coach and school chaplain.

Bill graduated with honours from the University of Life. As a young man he came to believe that he could make a difference for vulnerable people, so he set about supporting them with the help of his wife Bev. Their faith in God and commitment to Christianity provided them with the strength to assist others in becoming positive contributors to their communities.

This was evident in Bill's valued work at the Ballarat Specialist School. He treated all the students as equals, never focusing on a person's disabilities but rather on their abilities and on supporting them to succeed.

Bill's incredible ability to communicate with everyone has allowed him to connect with people from all walks of life. Bill's story hasn't been signed off on yet – he will keep on assisting his fellow human beings for as long as he can.

Enjoy the read and derive the benefits! Well done, Bill.

John Burt OAM, Former Principal
of the Ballarat Specialist School

Author's note

This book is about two things primarily. It is mostly about others, but it is also about my response to others. To the readers of this book, to quote one who was an unwitting mentor early in my life, 'You are special. There is no one else in the world like you. The world needs you. Your seeming deficits are your greatest assets. Your best education comes out of the School of Hard Knocks and the University of Adversity.' Because of that, if you have had a tough time in life, you are perhaps more qualified than anyone else, and you should use your qualifications to help others. Helping others is like throwing a boomerang, it comes back to you.

As I look back over what has been an incredibly fortunate life, despite an unfortunate start, I think of the encouraging and inspiring and motivational people who have cut across my path. I think that the positive seeds sown and watered by my mentors have helped me to reap a considerable harvest. Because of that, the driving force throughout my entire career has been my faith in the sowing and watering of seeds in people's lives.

The bestselling author Dale Carnegie wrote, 'People rarely succeed unless they have fun in what they are doing.' I've had fun for the whole fifty years plus of my career so far, and I think I've been reasonably successful. May you be too.

1

Losing more than an eye

I was born in the inner Melbourne suburb of Fitzroy. At that time, it was a very working-class area, and with the exception of the famous confectionary company MacRobertson's, which was so large it took up two blocks, it was not so much industrialised itself but surrounded by industry.

My mother, Lillian Mary, nee Skinner, and father, Robert (Bob) Thomas Turner, had a very turbulent relationship. Mum was religious; Dad wasn't. Mum didn't drink; Dad did. He wouldn't go to the Salvation Army Citadel with her; she wouldn't go to the pub with him. She would nag him: 'You don't do this.' 'You won't do that.' 'You're never home.' 'I've got to do everything on my own.' 'You like to be with your mates more than your kids and me.' My older sister Val used to joke that Mum was Phar Lap, the world's greatest nag, but I think she had reason to be. My father was grumpy and gruff. When he was angry, he made guttural sounds, pushed things out of the way and threw things around. He was like a keg of gunpowder with a short fuse, and it only took a small spark to make him explode.

Mum was sick and tired of Dad staying until closing time at the pub and not getting home for dinner or to give her a hand with us kids. It all came to a head one fateful night in 1944. We ate without him again, the meal consisting of the traditional meat and three vegies: mutton, pumpkin, peas and mashed potatoes. Wartime rationing of gas and electricity was still in force, so Mum put a plate over Dad's meal, placed it in the heated oven with the door slightly ajar and turned the gas off, hoping he would be home before his dinner went cold.

Three-year-old Val was usually very happy and talkative but was now very tired and miserable. I was eighteen months old and screaming out for attention from the high chair. Val was more direct. 'When is Daddy coming home?' she kept repeating like a parrot.

'He's never coming home!' Mum eventually shouted. Feeling overwhelmed, she threw his meal out.

Dad arrived home extremely late, having gone to a mate's house for more drinks after closing time. He was not only very intoxicated but also unremorseful and aggressive. Discovering that his meal had been thrown out, he picked up a carving knife from the sink and threw it at Mum. Instead of hitting her it hit me, piercing my left eye.

Self-preservation kicked in. Rather than worrying about me, Dad was so terrified of what might happen to him that he tried to prevent Mum from taking me to hospital. She finally managed to break away from him, screaming, with me bleeding profusely in her arms and bawling my eyes out, and Val hanging on to her skirt and screeching. She rushed out onto the street, hailed a taxi and took me to hospital. My eye had to be removed.

In fear of further violence, my mother didn't return to the house. She turned to the Salvation Army for help, and they placed us in emergency accommodation. Mum was pregnant with my sister Denice, who was born in the refuge in August 1944. My sisters and I were dedicated to God in the Salvation Army, their equivalent of infant baptism.

Mum didn't have Dad charged, and consequently he never faced court. However, their marriage broke up, and Mum never returned to the family home. We were destitute. Without money to pay for food or rent, Mum was supported by the Salvation Army for a considerable time. I had not only lost my eye but my father and family life as well.

~

In 1939, my father had enlisted in the army. His trade as a fitter and turner was considered an essential service at home, so he was not permitted to serve outside of Australia. He and his fellow reservist soldiers were deployed for the manufacturing of equipment for the war, working in munitions factories and on projects such as the construction of fuel storage tanks that were installed underground in Darwin. These men were widely despised and stigmatised by soldiers serving overseas, who spoke of them in derogatory terms. 'Chocos' meant they were like chocolate soldiers that would melt in the heat of battle, and 'bludgers on the Queen's shilling' meant they deserved pay in peacetime but not wartime. They were also called 'women' because single women between twenty and thirty were called up to replace men in factories and on farms.

After Mum left Dad, another serviceman entered our lives—a returned serviceman, one of the Anzacs who had fought in World War I. His name was Victor Hugh Sutcliffe, and he was to become my stepfather.

England was his country of origin, the Mother Country. He was born into a family of watchmakers in Burnley, Lancashire. His father was a very stern and fierce disciplinarian: when the boy stole some money out of the family jewellery shop, perhaps not for the first time, he got a horrific hiding. Though barely a teenager, he ran away from home and boarded a ship to Australia. Little is known of what he endured on the voyage. He worked as a farmhand on a sheep and wheat property in northern Victoria, and that made a pretty solid teenager out of him.

At eighteen he enlisted with the avalanche of over thirty-seven per cent of Australia's male population. He survived the horrors of Anzac Cove on the Gallipoli Peninsula, in an area known as 'Hell Spit'. Of the 60,000 Australians who fought at Gallipoli, 7594 were killed and 26,000 wounded, many of them solid teenagers like him.

From 1917, the Soldier Settlement Scheme offered farmland with long-term and very low interest repayments to returned servicemen. Victor bought a block near Mildura. When he purchased a team of bullocks to work his block, he met my grandfather Bill Skinner, a bullock breeder and breaker from Gippsland, and through him my mother.

Many of the returned servicemen taking part in the scheme were totally inexperienced at farming, and the blocks of land were often too small to produce enough income. The price of farm commodities fell throughout the 1920s, and after the Wall Street Crash in 1929 there was the Great Depression during the thirties to contend with, as the export of wool and wheat—the main source of our nation's income—dropped dramatically. One-third of participants in the scheme walked away from their farms never to return, including Victor, some time during the 1930s. His first wife died by suicide, and their six kids were placed in children's homes. All of them were to remain permanently scarred from their time there, some worse than others.

Incredibly, Victor re-enlisted at the start of World War II. Although the maximum age for enlistment was forty and he was forty-one, he was nevertheless accepted and served overseas once more, this time in the Airforce, in transport. He had a major truck accident towards the end of the war, however, and was repatriated back to Australia and hospitalised in Melbourne. After recuperation he commenced employment as a toolmaker at the Turner Manufacturing Company. A bit ironic because my father's surname was Turner!

Mum had her own sad circumstances. Her mother, a Wallace, Grandpa Skinner's first wife, died of cancer when Mum was only seven years old. Not long afterwards her father walked into their home with a woman and said, 'This is your new mother.' Mum hadn't adequately grieved the loss of Grandma Wallace and couldn't take to her stepmother at all, constantly clashing with her. At fourteen Mum left home to work as a domestic in the north-western Victorian town of Horsham. Grandma Wallace had been a devout member of the Salvation

Army, and Mum followed in her footsteps, attending the local citadel whenever she could.

It would be easy to judge Grandpa Skinner without knowing the great difficulties of those days, when there wasn't the welfare support that there is today. Fearing that he would lose his six children, he went with the most pragmatic solution: he remarried quickly. In fact, his first wife, Mum's mother, and my Grandma Wallace, had been a war widow with three young children when she married him; her first husband had died at Anzac Cove, while Victor Sutcliffe survived.

Mum never bonded with Grandpa Skinner again, and in later life she said that she had longed to do so. Victor was twenty-five years older than my mother and perhaps in marrying someone her father's age, she was inadvertently marrying her father—not uncommon.

~

When Mum married Victor, despite already having three children of her own, she made sure all of his kids came out of the children's homes. His two daughters, Gladys and Eunice, were fostered out. Of his four sons, Victor Junior joined the navy and lived away, and Tom, Ellis and Maurice lived with us at various times. We didn't have much to do with the girls, but Mum accepted the boys as just part of our family. Eight children were born into our family by my stepfather, five girls and three boys. In order of birth they were Eddie, Gordon, Jeannie, Gladys, Norma, Carmel (who was born at home and sadly died three months later), Lila and Ivan. For whatever reason, the fourth child born to Mum was named Gladys also. Perhaps calling another child Gladys was my stepfather's way of keeping his first Gladys, who he had lost through her being fostered out.

We lived in Millgrove at Grundy's Sawmill, where my stepfather worked and where our house was located. Grandfather Skinner managed Grundy's sawmill as well as a number of other sawmills in other areas and arranged the job for my stepfather there.

Millgrove was a picturesque and tiny town in the Yarra Ranges some sixty kilometres east of Melbourne. Situated on the banks of the famous Upper Yarra River with an abundance of trout fish and towering mountain gum trees. It was located at the base of Mount Little Joe with a train line running just above the main road on the north side of the township. The prominent shops were the general store, greengrocers and newsagents. Grundys sawmill was on a large acreage with hundreds of felled trees stockpiled for milling. My memories of our house are that it was a plain cabin-type structure, but large enough to accommodate all the children, although as was common then, some of the children slept together. My stepfather was a sawyer, responsible for pushing logs through large sawblades and sizing boards for housing.

For whatever reason, my stepfather found it difficult to accept me. Perhaps in his eyes I was a reflection of him as a young person, and he didn't like what he saw. He became the savage disciplinarian that his father had been to him, at least to me—I think I became his whipping boy. He felt he had to give me a hiding regularly, so much so that often when he passed me he would hit me behind the ears, saying, 'For the things I've missed you doing.'

By the early 1950s, Eddie, three years younger than me—had become my playmate and closest companion. We'd get up to mischief around town and lose track of time, which meant we were regularly late for dinner. I was mostly to blame and got punished by my stepfather accordingly. In the early days he would grab me, throw me into a bedroom and leave me there without dinner, but it wasn't long before he began to belt me extensively with a razor strop kept nearby for that purpose. The more he punished me, the more cunning and resilient I became. Having returned home with Eddie after yet another adventure, I would go into hiding, sometimes all night until Victor left for work the next morning. I missed a lot of meals and a lot of school, but I also missed a lot of beltings.

Like an elephant, my stepfather did not forget and would try to punish me later if he could. A heavy man in his fifties, he was too slow to catch me, so he used two of his sons, Ellis and Tom, as his legs—or, as I used to think, as dogs to round me up like a wild animal. Tom was a kind and caring person, but he was fearful of his father; on a number of occasions he refused to participate and remonstrated with Victor, so he was beaten too. Ellis, on the other hand, was cruel, callous and ever anxious to please his father.

Tom and Ellis worked in tandem: one would head me off while the other would follow on behind and try to corner me. They only occasionally caught me, but woe betide me when they did. After being dragged kicking, screaming and punching into a bedroom, I would be held by them and belted mercilessly by my stepfather. I would drop to the floor in a foetal position, but that was no help to me, because he would then start kicking into me, all the time swearing at me and telling me what a terrible kid I was. 'You are no good and never will be any good,' he would keep repeating. I noticed that when adults fought each other, he would say it was the height of cowardice for them to resort to kicking.

So that the belting would cause more pain, Victor would pull my shirt or jumper up to my shoulders and expose bare flesh. Wild West films were all the rage in that era, and the vision of a tough cowboy biting on a bullet when he had an operation without anaesthetic was vivid in my mind. I once tried stuffing part of my shirt into my mouth and clamping my teeth on it to stifle my screams and deaden the extreme pain, but it didn't work. My stepfather became even more sadistic, saying, 'Pull that out of your mouth or I'll pull your teeth out with a pair of pliers.' In no doubt that he would, I quickly complied.

The more I attempted to evade my hunters, the more severe my beatings became. My back was left badly abraded, but scabs were barely allowed to form before I was belted again. There was a 'cure' for this, an archaic, barbaric cure: salt. After one of my beatings, Victor and my stepbrothers restrained me again while they rubbed salt into my wounds. As bad as the pain of being belted and kicked was, that faded into insignificance compared to the pain of salt penetrating my broken flesh. It felt as though boiling water or acid was being poured over my back. The pain was so intense, so extensive and deep, that it literally took my breath away, and I fell down, believing I would die. I think this worried Ellis and Tom, and maybe Victor momentarily, because my stepbrothers immediately took their hands off me, and my stepfather stepped back, looking shocked. Who knows, maybe he had a flashback to receiving similar treatment on board the ship to Australia. But if he did, it certainly didn't deter him from further salt treatments.

Although the pain seemed to last forever, it probably lasted for about ten to fifteen minutes. After a while scar tissue started to harden on my back, which meant the beltings didn't feel so painful. I steeled myself and was determined to win the battle of the beatings.

I tried another tack: screaming blue murder, which caused the whole household and especially Mum to become distraught. She would rush into the bedroom and try to pull my stepfather away from me, shouting at him to stop hitting me or I would be seriously hurt. While my stepbrothers were still holding me, Victor would turn on her, belting her as well. She would cower like a maltreated dog, then cry uncontrollably. This hurt me more than my own beatings, and it made me even angrier. Sometimes after my stepfather did this, he would suddenly storm away to have a cigarette and a beer, shouting at me as he went, 'You caused this, you worthless mongrel of a kid. You'll keep!' And keep I did, like a carcase in a coolroom waiting to be cut up.

Despite Mum being emotionally overwhelmed at times like this she had an incredible resilience. In the aftermath of her husband's attacks, she would burst into song. It was obviously a source of great comfort for her and helped her to settle down. I would hear her singing old hymns, often through sobs and considerable pain. Her voice would become stronger with every line. Her favourite song in tough times was 'Lily of the Valley', with its opening line 'I have found a friend in Jesus'. In lighter moments she would burst into Irish and Scottish ballads such as 'When Irish Eyes Are Smiling' and 'The Bonnie Banks o' Loch Lomond'.

I was forever parodying things and I couldn't help myself with this. I started singing, 'You're the Lily of the valley', referring to Mum, whose name, of course, was Lillian. Mum didn't take kindly to me mocking a spiritual song she so valued. 'That's bad, Billy. It's blasphemous,' she said. 'Don't ever say that again!' I didn't know what 'blasphemy' meant then, but I knew well enough not to try that on again.

Although Mum had been a devout member of the Salvation Army since she was a teenager, I couldn't embrace Christianity. Having witnessed and experienced brutal domestic violence, I couldn't accept that a powerful and loving God would allow such suffering. But even though I professed to be a bitter atheist, I could never get past the inexplicable power of Mum's singing.

∼

My stepfather repeatedly told me that he couldn't stand the sight of me. He devised a new bedroom for me outside the house: a six by four-foot trailer at the back of an old Dodge utility, covered in sheet metal with the original tailgate still intact. It was freezing cold in winter and stifling hot in summer.

One night, I slammed the tailgate shut as I crawled into my bedroom. It clattered and clanged like the steel door of a prison cell. The trailer rocked in the wind, and the old leaf springs squeaked. In my mind they weren't springs, though: they were the excited squeaks of rats the size of wombats realising that their supper had arrived. I froze in fear, then double-checked to make sure the tailgate was secure and that there were no holes in the canopy. The darkness under the blankets only exacerbated my fear. The giant rats were now rocking the trailer. Their squeaking was getting louder and louder. They were trying to dislodge the floor-boards to get at me from underneath. I curled myself into a tighter ball, wrapping the blankets around me. *They will never know I'm here,* I thought. *They won't be able to get me.*

It was still dark when I woke up. Something was rubbing my shoulder and side. I stiffened. Was a giant rat feeling for the meatiest parts of my body?

A voice suddenly sounded. I shrieked and rolled away, hitting the trailer canopy very hard. 'It's all right, Billy, it's me,' said a silky-smooth voice, low and syrupy. It was the voice of an older stepbrother who worked away and returned home periodically on weekends. A memory of him brutally beheading an unwanted litter of pups flashed into my mind. 'Are you lonely out here, Billy?'

Lonely? I was an eight-year-old kid, scared stiff and frightened out of my wits from time to time, including that very moment. There was nothing to offset my loneliness. When you are constantly beaten and bullied, told you are stupid and no good, and continu-ously rejected, loneliness is a normal part of life.

I was pressing myself into the side of the canopy, afraid and bewildered. The blankets were being lifted up behind me. A warm body was pressing into my back. My shoulders and back were being gently rubbed. Despite still being scared, I was now relaxing— in fact, I was going to sleep.

But then I was wide awake again, because I could feel some-thing greasy between the back of my legs. My shoulders were being held tight.

'Don't worry, Billy,' my stepbrother said, pressing tightly against me.

12

Whatever the greasy stiff thing between my legs was, it was going faster and faster. His breathing was getting heavier and heavier. Finally he stopped, and something was oozing against my legs.

'Are you awake?' he asked.

I could hardly not be.

'Here, wipe yourself.' In the darkness he placed a rag into my hands. He stayed in my bed a little while, pressed against me. I was so frightened and confused. As he got up to leave he handed me something else. 'Don't lose it. It's worth a lot. Don't tell anyone about this. I'll give you more later.' I discovered it was a ten-shilling note, a fortune to me.

When I went into the house the next morning, my stepbrother was there telling my mother and stepfather that he had given me some money to be good and help around the place.

'Well, you're wasting your money,' my stepfather said. 'He couldn't be good if he tried, and he wouldn't work in an iron lung.'

I smarted at that. I had already established a solid work ethic, stacking timber at another sawmill after school and on weekends.

'Well, you never know,' my abuser said. 'It's a good incentive. I'll give him another chance when I'm home next time.'

And that's what happened for the next two years. Whenever he was home he would appear in the trailer in the middle of the night or early in the morning. The abuse only got more painful and more revolting.

~

My first artificial eye was a glass one that I broke at an early age. My stepfather said, 'I'll be buggered if I'm buying you another one. They cost a fortune, and you'll only break that as well.' So I attended school, played sport, and walked around town with a grotesque empty eye socket. I was regularly bullied, often called 'freak' and 'retard', and forever getting into fights. I believe the main reason I was bullied was because of what I call 'the wounded chicken' syndrome: when a chicken has an obvious injury such as a broken leg, other chickens will peck at it, and if it is not taken away they will ultimately kill it. My missing eye made me a wounded chicken for all my primary school years.

At home I was a very scared nine-year-old who continued to be banished to my trailer each evening after dinner and would try to get back into the house at my peril. As I lay wrapped in my blankets one stormy night, the rain on the canopy was like machine-gun fire, and the fierce wind made me imagine that a dinosaur had the trailer in its mouth. After what seemed like an eternity, I went to sleep. In the early hours of the morning, I woke to the wind still roaring, and through it I thought I heard the squawking of a baby magpie. *Surely not*, I told myself. The sound continued on and off until I fell asleep again.

When I got up and went inside to have breakfast and prepare for school, I thought I must have dreamt of the magpie because I couldn't hear any squawking. But it was hard to hear anything over the ringing of a large circular saw that reverberated in the distance. That sound was the reason why I had got out of bed: the signal that my stepfather had gone to work at the sawmill.

Mum was always very talkative over breakfast without the combativeness between me and my stepfather. She was interested in how I had fared during the night. I never let on how scared

I really was at times or that terrible things had been happening to me. However, that morning I did say that I thought I'd heard a baby magpie.

'Come with me,' Mum said.

I followed her out to the back of the house. In a large cage that had previously housed a white cockatoo, an open-mouthed, hungry, squawking baby magpie greeted me. It looked more like a half-plucked quail than a magpie. Mum had rescued the baby magpie when she heard its loud, plaintive cry early in the morning. The cockatoo had been a rescue bird also and I think Mum was happy to see the empty cage used again for that purpose. It was let out of the cage accidently by one of the children, never to be seen again.

That bird became my first pet—not by choice or by design, but because I continued to look after her and became very attached to her. I named the bird 'Heckle' after one of the postwar magpie cartoon characters Heckle and Jeckle. I should have named her 'Angel', considering what she came to mean to me. There's no doubt she wouldn't have survived without being rescued. In time she was as dependent on me as she would have been on her natural parents—and just as demanding.

When I first started trying to warble like a magpie, Heckle would put her head on one side and then the other whimsically, taking it in. Sometimes she would shake her head in disbelief at what I was warbling about and slowly walk away. Maybe my attempted warble was swearing in magpie language! She gradually accepted, however, that I was trying to communicate with her, and she would look at me almost with reverence—at least I told myself that. I tried out my warbling on wild magpies, and it stopped them in their tracks when they were dive-bombing in nesting season. Who knows what I was really saying to them, but at least they came to recognise that I was no threat to them or their young.

Mum began to call me 'Birdman', and I soon became generally known as 'the Birdman'. This gave me some prestige and status, certainly some self-confidence, and the awareness that I was good at something and loved by someone, if only of the feathered variety. A few students at my school were enthralled by my warbling and tried it themselves. Sadly, it didn't take long before the bullies started to chase the magpies away and cast aspersions on my masculinity because of my soft side, calling me 'the weird Birdman' and telling me that only girls played with birds. The girls took notice of me, though, so I knew I was on a winner. I was able to do something that none of the other kids could do. I found that 'Birdman' was no insult but rather a compliment, although it got me into even more fights.

2

Hitting back

There is no excuse for crime, but poverty can be a powerfully seductive motive. When your clothing and your footwear are torn and threadbare, and you are being ridiculed and ostracised, and there is no such thing as pocket money because your family is poor, crime can be very tempting, Not only was I poor, but I was also being sexually abused by my stepbrother, who continued to give me shillings. Despite the horror of my abuse, perhaps he helped to whet my appetite for money. I now believe that this was one of his ploys. I yielded to the temptation to become a shoplifter at just nine years of age.

I had been shoplifting from a particular business for a long time. Then one day a a hand was placed firmly on my shoulder, and I froze. I was expecting to be savagely swung around and severely beaten, which was common in that era, or to be taken home to my parents, which would have been worse than being dragged down to the police station. Any beating from the business owner would have paled into insignificance next to what my stepfather would have done.

Instead, the firm hand on my shoulder turned me gently around, and I looked into the face of a wonderfully understanding and tolerant man. The business owner asked me how long I had been stealing from him and by what means. When I told him the truth, instead of castigating me—or worse—he congratulated me. 'Son, you're good,' he said. 'You've been very cunning and clever. I thought I could very quickly catch anyone who stole from me, but you have outsmarted me.'

I was flabbergasted. It was amazing—here I was being congratulated for my expertise in committing crime.

'You are very gifted, son, but what you need to do is use your gifts for positive purposes rather than for negative ones. Help people rather than steal from them. Promise me you'll do that and never do this again, and I won't tell your parents or the police. Deal?'

We shook hands.

Other early experiences with adults weren't so positive. I had quickly learnt that my teachers seemed oblivious not only to the domestic violence but also to the bullying. They were always concerned about what had happened, not why it had happened—just 'Billy Sutcliffe was in a fight again', rather than the cause.

Our brains are wired to make us flee, fight or freeze when we're attacked, and I was a fighter with words and fists. A student in the grade above mine regularly came to my rescue when I got into scuffles at school. On one occasion an older student was name-calling me because of my eye, so I flew at him, punching his stomach and chest. He got me down on the ground and was sitting on me before my rescuer intervened. As the fight was broken up, I shouted, 'I would bite your balls off except you don't have any, you girl!'

I must have worn a track to the headmaster's office, where he would lecture me about the consequences of fighting and then belt me on the hand with a leather strap. I was also made to do manual labour around the school, a punishment intended to keep me away from the kids I had been fighting with.

I would get pretty assertive with the headmaster, telling him that it wasn't fair for me to be punished. I might have started the fight, but I hadn't started the name-calling. 'Anyway,' I would add, 'you can't hurt me with that stupid strap.' Then he would try even harder to hurt me, giving me extra cuts for good measure. And he did manage to hurt me, especially on cold days, but I would never let on—not a very smart move!

His parting advice would often be, 'Bill, you've got to learn to not take offence to words. Say to yourself, "Sticks and stones may break my bones, but names will never hurt me".'

Sure, I would think to myself, *you ask me not to be bothered by words, but you obviously have been—you've just given me extra cuts for using words you didn't like.*

On the one hand I was a fighter who stood up for myself, while on the other I was very sensitive and deeply affected by bullying. My unjust treatment by school staff fertilised my immense feelings of rejection, which constantly plagued me. At times I would get deeply depressed. Someone had told me that sick old dogs sometimes wander away and lie down to die, and I began to think of doing this.

I was just nine years old when negative thoughts escalated in my mind for days and drove me into a bottomless dark pit that I could see no way out of. I found myself walking up and down alongside the railway line at the foot of Mount Little Joe, where Eddie and I had carried out many exploits, and where I had lain down in the bushes many times and shed many a despairing tear because of the abuse.

This time I lay across the train tracks. *What filthy scum I am*, I thought. *What a vile wicked person. I deserve to go to hell. The world would be a better place without me.*

I could hear the train in the distance. *Wooo! Woooo!* It was getting closer and closer, louder and louder. I was crying inconsolably, not wanting to live but not wanting to die. The wheels were screeching, skidding, as the driver desperately applied the brakes.

The words of the shopkeeper came to my mind: 'Son, you're good. Help people.'

I rolled off the track in an instant. Cursing from the train driver followed me—little did he know why I'd done it. I ran as far away as I could and fell in a heap, sobbing my heart out. The shopkeeper who I had stolen from had saved me.

~

Life wasn't all gloom and doom. A great part of my in-built survival mechanism was escapism, which took on all sorts of entertaining forms. I would devise satisfying ways of getting back at my abusers, even in my sleep.

Just after I got Heckle, I started dreaming that I was a collared sparrowhawk. This bird was my type of hunter, as it soared above everything, in total control. Not only was it very fast and cunning, but it was a master of disguise as well: its colours of white, slate-grey, black, yellow and light and dark brown made it almost indistinguishable from its habitat.

In my dream I would just happen to be around when one of my abusers went to our outside toilet. I would swoop out of the sky like a lightning strike. Only the sun shining on my feathers and the swoosh of my wings when I stalled to drop my payload gave any indication of a pending attack. But by the time they heard the swoosh of my wings, I was aiming and firing. Too late! Bullseye! I always hit my target. *Splat!* Right in the hair or on the face. They would wipe it off, swear at me, and try to throw things at me, but all in vain.

As I swooped and dive-bombed my abusers, their eyes would dart left and right, up and down, in fearful apprehension. I could always get them to run away in panic, shielding their faces as I sped towards them. Soon enough they would trip over and twist their ankles—then they were sitting ducks.

Being the Bomber Birdman was so real to me and so entertaining that I would often wake myself up at night laughing my head off and congratulating myself after yet another successful sortie. I wanted my abusers to get a taste of their own medicine.

~

My little brother Eddie was still my shadow. It's a wonder he survived because in following me he lived on the edge also, and faced a lot of danger. We shared many adventures and had plenty of fun. Sometimes we stole vegetables from a neighbour's garden, and occasionally we surfed on logs as they were being dragged by draught horses at the sawmill where Victor worked, imagining the logs were surfboards. I'm ashamed to say we would often climb trees to raid bird's nests, obtaining eggs for our substantial collection; we would carefully prick a hole in each of the eggs and blow the insides out so there wouldn't be a rotten smell in our room. Fishing in the Upper Yarra River was also a popular pursuit. Eddie was a much better fisherman than I was, having the patience to sit down with hook and line and wait endlessly for a bite. I preferred attaching a lure to a line, then watching it spin and shine in the water as I pulled it along.

Wherever Eddie and I went, we seemed to attract incidents, some funny, some serious. On one occasion when Eddie was only about four years old, we were out fishing with the family at the Yarra when he caught a small brown frog. He was as proud as Punch, standing open-mouthed alongside me and Mum on the riverbank saying, 'Look, look!' All of a sudden the frog jumped into his mouth. He gulped in surprise and fright—and swallowed it! Perhaps that's where the idiom 'a frog in my throat' originated.

Weekends were often taken up by drunken parties, and one such occasion took place at a neighbour's home on the side of Mount Little Joe. Eddie and I were six and nine years old respectively. The beer was flowing from an eighteen-gallon keg into jugs that were poured into glasses. There was little supervision of the children—in fact, as the night wore on and the adults got more intoxicated, supervision became non-existent. Eddie and I were

helping ourselves to glasses of beer and smoking hand-rolled cig-
arettes that were lying around. I found I hated the taste of tobacco,
though, and didn't continue to smoke.

There was a steep incline of a couple of hundred yards up to the
house from the main road that connected Millgrove to Warburton.
The Melbourne railway line ran past at about the halfway mark.
Quite late at night, whether by accident or intent, Eddie and I found
ourselves rolling down the rough driveway from the house towards
the train tracks and the road. Eddie must have been frightened out
of his wits, because I was terrified as I started to gain momentum.
It's a wonder we weren't killed from head injuries alone as we hit
the tracks on the way down.

We veered off the road into a clump of bushes, breaking our fall
and possibly saving our lives. Although badly shaken and extensively scratched and bruised, we collapsed into a hysterical heap,
laughing our heads off. Sadly at that very young age we were quite
intoxicated, which had probably relaxed us enough to prevent
serious injuries, but on the other hand was most likely the cause of
the stupid, dangerous act in the first place.

~

I led Eddie astray with an act of sabotage. We would steal potatoes
from a greengrocer, take them up Mount Little Joe and throw them
at vehicles below on the Millgrove–Warburton Road. We were
lucky that cars and trucks tended to go much slower in those days,
and no one was killed or seriously injured as far as I know. This
activity came to an abrupt end when an angry motorist screeched
his car to a halt after it was hit by a potato I threw. He flung his

door open and looked up the hill, seeming to glare directly at me. Then he started to run towards us. He had no hope of catching us, as we knew Mount Little Joe and its hidey-holes like the back of our hands. Nevertheless we hid for hours in fear that he might be waiting for us.

You would think I learnt my lesson from that, but no. Not long afterwards, I decided to attempt to derail a train. For whatever reason, Eddie wasn't with me on this occasion, and maybe deep down I didn't want him to be. I might have been protecting him from the potential repercussions of such a terrible act.

I was walking alongside the railway line, gathering objects to put on the tracks, when I needed to go to the toilet in a hurry. There were fairly dense bushes nearby, so I crouched down in them, took off my belt and pulled down my shorts.

I hadn't counted on what happened next: the hoot of a passenger train coming around the bend frightened the life out of me. Standing bolt upright, I pulled up my shorts and ran for my life, crashing through the bushes until the train was well out of sight and sound. I had visions of passengers packed in carriages as tall as houses, and all of these people peering down and laughing at me.

Then it dawned on me: my belt! I had left it behind in the panic. That belt had been a gift for my ninth birthday. It had a gleaming Scout buckle. Thoughts of it linking me with the objects left alongside the tracks caused my mind to run rampant with fear. What if the train guard had already reported his sighting of the material and me to the Warburton police at the next train stop, and the officers were on their way?

Racing down the hill and over the road to my prison-bedroom in the trailer, I never looked back. And I never tried that horrifying act of vandalism again.

A piece of string did the job of holding up my shorts, and invisible person that I was, no one seemed to notice that my belt with the Scout buckle was missing. No one, that is, except Eddie. After a number of days he asked me why I wasn't wearing it. 'Can't find it, mate,' I said. He never asked me again.

The belt kept coming back to haunt me, though. Because my sexual abuser had given it to me, the thought of it tormented me for a long time. I was glad I had lost it—and yet I hadn't really lost it. It was a reminder of how doubly bad I was, or so I saw it at the time, for being involved in unspeakable stuff with my abuser and for trying to do potentially deadly stuff to a train full of people. The memory of the belt kept adding to my belief that I had not only allowed my abuser to commit sordid acts on me, but I had also taken money for this. That my abuser had managed to transfer to me a sense of blame shows how expert he was at emotional abuse as well.

∼

There was one other incident involving the railway when I was nine years of age. It happened when my stepfather took me on a train to visit Melbourne. I don't remember taking any other trips alone with him, and I believe he brought me along so I would be an aid to him when the inevitable occurred. I have no memories of where we went or what we did in Melbourne, but I do have vivid memories of the journey back.

It had been a hot day, and my stepfather, a heavy drinker at the best of times, was quite intoxicated when we boarded the train home. As usual he carried a brown Gladstone leather bag with a couple of large bottles of Victoria Bitter beer inside. The Gladstone was a common bag for men to carry in those days, classless in as much as doctors carried them as well as sportsmen and wharfies and the average Joe Blow.

The more my stepfather drank, the louder his voice became and the more embarrassed I was to be associated with him. When he went to the toilet, I moved into another carriage and sat alone, pretending I didn't know him. But that just made matters worse. When he returned to his seat and discovered me missing, he started calling out for me. 'Billy? Billy, where are you?' His voice started as a shout and became a roar as he lurched along the train trying to find me. Aggression took over, and he cursed and swore, making threats about what he would do to me after we got home.

I pressed myself against the window with my back to the passage-way. A woman came to sit alongside me and put an arm around my shoulder, pretending I was with her in order to hide me as my stepfather continued his rampage. In my thinking I had now gone much too far to reveal myself to him. At every station he thought I had left the train and was on the platform and would endeavour to get off to look for me, shouting my name more loudly each time. Unfortunately he always made it back onto the train.

It seemed like it took forever to arrive at Millgrove Station. I rushed out the door, intending to run home and go into hiding for the night, but all of a sudden I was under the train. In my frantic haste I had slipped between the platform and the carriage, crashing onto the tracks. The train hooted, about to complete the final leg of its journey to Warburton. As I struggled to climb out, the steel wheels faced me like circular saws about to rip into a log and cut it in half.

Then I heard an urgent shrill female voice. 'Don't move the train! *Don't move the train, there's a kid under it!*'

Eileen Burgess had just become my hero. The guard got a message to the driver in time to save me. I was relatively unscathed physically, but mentally and emotionally I was very shaken. I had recurring nightmares of the incident for a long time, and I would shudder every time I heard a train horn. Although I received the usual verbal tirade from my stepfather, he showed he had some heart because I was spared any other punishment due to my near-death experience.

3

Proving them wrong

Nineteen fifty-three was my tenth year but felt like my twentieth. It was the year I was liberated from my trailer prison—the year I slept in a normal bedroom again, I had shifted with my family from Millgrove to just outside Wycheproof on the west side. We had gone from sawmilling to farming; from the mountainous, heavily timbered, wet, cold country of the Yarra Valley in eastern Victoria to the billiard-table flat, hot, dry, tree-razed wheat country of northern Victoria. Due to his involvement in the Soldier Settlement Scheme, my stepfather had contacts in Wycheproof. He share-farmed a thousand acres and grew wheat, barley and oats. The premium barley was used to make beer. Share-farming meant cultivating and harvesting the entire property plus running sheep and cattle and sharing the profits with the owner. The farmhouse was typical of that era: a wooden structure with verandahs on every side and four bedrooms, very different to our cabin in Millgrove.

It was about ten miles from Wycheproof and we caught a school bus at the front of the property to go to school. The township was built on each side of a railway line that ran through the town, and while consisting of the normal range of stores and amenities, its large agricultural business denoted the rural area that it was.

On the edge of the township was Mount Wycheproof, the world's smallest mountain. It was like a pimple on a pumpkin. Although a thousand feet above sea level, it was only forty-three yards above the surrounding countryside. It later became famous for the King of the Mountain contest in which contestants would run from the main street to the summit carrying a 154-pound bag of wheat on their back.

In the competitive environment of a hard-working farming community, I was driven to prove my stepfather wrong. I strove to prove that I could be the best worker there was. The sad thing is that whenever I succeeded, he failed to acknowledge it or gave me a backhanded compliment. He would keep me home from school to help him with his job, saying, 'I'm glad you're not at school today and giving a hand. I don't want Eddie to miss school—he's got a good head on his shoulders.'

Despite this, at school I was developing a number of talents. I had joined a book club and started to read prolifically, mainly about Biggles, Buck Rogers, the world wars, flight, and science fiction. Reading aloud became my great passion, and the worlds of my literary heroes became a great source of escapism and a stimulus for creativity. I started to write poems and short stories, and I loved to read them out the front of the class during our composition lessons. Then I would read them to my brothers and sisters, ultimately driving them mad. I would also read extracts from books, brochures and newspapers to them—almost anything that could be read!

My all-time favourite story was one from a school reader, Henry Lawson's 'The Loaded Dog'. It struck a very familiar chord with me. Although it was about three goldminers—Dave, Jim and Andy—and their retriever dog Tommy, in my mind it was about me, my main bullies at school, and sweet revenge.

The miners had been using a stick of gelignite to catch fish. They were chatting around a camp fire on the outskirts of town when Tommy sauntered innocently over to the gelignite stick, picked it up in his mouth and, like a good retriever, trotted over to his masters—dragging the fuse through the fire and igniting it. The men ran for their lives, and Tommy followed one of them towards the pub. Cutting across the retriever's path, however, was his nemesis: a yellow mongrel dog and his pack of followers.

Yellow was forever bullying Tommy, snapping and snarling at him, and snatching any bones he had in his mouth when caught unawares. This occasion was no exception. Tommy's prize this time, however, was wrapped in canvas and glowing at one end. Yellow greedily clamped the explosive device in his teeth and pranced proudly under the pub, his pack blindly following him.

Boom! Yellow was blown to smithereens, and all of his followers were badly maimed. The pub kitchen, fortunately unoccupied, was sent upwards in a thousand pieces, and sausages, steak, bacon and chops rained down. Manna from heaven! When the dust settled, and before the three shocked mates regained their equilibrium, Tommy was having the feed of his life at Yellow's expense.

What a boon for my burgeoning creativity. My mind ran rampant, and my composition class couldn't come around quickly enough. I was very excited as I stood proudly in front of the class reading my rendition of 'The Loaded Dog'.

When I read out the name of my main schoolyard bully in place of Yellow and six others as the pack of dogs, a real explosion occurred—one of anger, humiliation and embarrassment from my bullies, and disappointment and dismay from my teacher. Then World War III erupted. Pieces of writing slate and chalk were thrown, and swear words were shouted and screamed, and finally the teacher roared, '*Quiet! Stop!*'

All eyes were directed at me. Burning into me. Accusing me. Applauding me. I was grinning like a Cheshire cat who had got all the cream. It had been a mighty few moments of getting even— not that my teacher thought so, but many in the class who had been bullied by the same pack did.

'Bill, off to the headmaster!' said the teacher. 'He's *not* going to be very pleased!' And he wasn't. I got a lecture and a few cuts with the strap, although I sensed some sympathy and a bit of restraint with the force of the belting.

The bullies had a go at me after school, throwing stones and trying to catch me, but they didn't succeed. This significantly broke the back of their bullying of me, and of others. Suddenly it was realised that I was both a fighter and a thinker, and I gained a lot of allies.

By this time I was reasonably good at most sport, and I was especially keen on cricket at school. One of my teachers was keen on it too, and his surname was Godfrey, which brought to mind

England's test wicketkeeper, Godfrey Evans, considered to be the best in the world at that time. Mr Godfrey encouraged me to be the wicketkeeper in the school team and to model my keeping on his namesake. I loved the position. It required great courage and hand-eye coordination, and I wanted to prove I had those attributes. Mr Godfrey told me that I did. His encouragement of me established a real rapport between us and I started to open up to him and confide in him a little bit.

Mr Godfrey was one of the few teachers who showed genuine interest in the why, not just the what, of my behaviour. He was also one of the few teachers who had ever shown much interest in me; he wanted to know why I had explosive reactions from time to time, rather than just saying, as most did, 'Sutcliffe's at it again'. He questioned me about my home life, and while I wasn't particularly forthcoming with details of my abuse, he seemed to read between the lines. He told me, 'It's no wonder you fly off the handle sometimes. I would too probably, under the same circumstances, especially when you're getting picked on over your eye.'

After 'The Loaded Dog' incident, Mr Godfrey took me aside one day and said, 'Bill, I've been thinking about your situation. I reckon what you've got to do, more than anything, is to prove people wrong. All those people you've told me about who have put you down over the years and said you'll never amount to anything— prove them wrong! Otherwise you'll play into their hands, and they'll say, "I told you so". You've got a good mind, an analytical mind, a creative mind, and your "Loaded Dog" rewrite proved that. You're also good at sport. Be the best you can be at everything you do, and you will certainly prove people wrong.'

I have been such a driven person throughout my life partly because of those seeds sown by Mr Godfrey.

~

Having learnt to drive a tractor at about the age of ten, I must have been only eleven when my skills were put to the test.

My stepfather had purchased a gleaming black Studebaker with doors that opened backwards rather than forwards. He brought it home and displayed it proudly. All the children, including me, sat in it and went for a ride. He then decided to take it for a test drive, alone on the Narraport Road, to see how fast it could go.

Victor was going pretty fast when the car hit a pothole and became airborne. While it was off the ground the steering wheel must have been turned inadvertently, because when the car hit the road again it lurched sharply to one side and rolled over a number of times.

My stepfather lost consciousness and had no recollection of what happened next. He wasn't thrown out of the car despite there not being seatbelts in those days. Although he was badly battered and bruised, he didn't break any bones. The Studebaker was a write-off, however. My stepfather was quite shaken by the accident and remarkably his attitude to me softened somewhat. He was now dependent on me.

The paddocks had to be cultivated after a downpour in preparation for sowing, and the window of opportunity couldn't be missed. I was kept home from school to drive the tractor for the cultivating, which allowed me to prove I was good for something after all. Unwittingly, my stepfather was another of my greatest motivators.

~

From an early age I was very industrious and had become proficient at a number of farm jobs, such as sewing up bags of cereal grain, milking cows, and building and maintaining fences. A year after I left school at age twelve, I took up an extremely smelly farm job. No, it wasn't the job of a nightman: it was a very profitable family business plucking dead wool off sheep. It involved my stepfather, Mum and I, and Eddie. Val and Denice, the two older sisters, stayed back at the house looking after three of the four youngest siblings aged from eight to three, Gordon, Gladys and Norma.

The price of wool had risen so high that the phrase 'Australia rides on the sheep's back' was true once again. Because of that, farmers didn't bother collecting wool from sheep that died—and there were many dead sheep. My stepfather would drive Mum and Eddie into the paddocks and then wait while they plucked the dead wool and loaded it into his vehicle. Jeannie, who was only seven, insisted that she try and help, and was able to pour some of the grain into the bags, but understandably tired out pretty quickly. Ellis gave a hand also when he could, but kept getting roused on by his father for not filling the bags enough before sewing them up so didn't stay around long. Maybe that's how he got out of it! Although I was relieved he was there to shift the bags, I dreaded him being there because he parroted his father's put-downs of me. I would collect wool in wheat bags and cart them, two at a time, on the rack on the back of my Malvern Star bike. In all fairness to my stepfather, he wasn't able to assist with any of the bag-sewing work because he was sixty-one and twenty-five years older than my mother and had a major back injury.

After the sheep had been dead for two or three days, the skin would turn green and the wool would just fall out. The residue and smell would constantly be on your hands and under your finger-nails, and using gloves for such purposes was unheard of then. Mum's answer to comments about that was, 'The sheep smell bad but the money smells good.' The work was probably unhealthy, but at least lanolin is good for the skin.

Until the 1960s, farmers still put wheat and other cereal grains into bags on their farms. Bag sewing was a much more pleasant job. But being quite an arduous task it required strong fingers. The bags were sewn up in the paddocks. Full bags of wheat weighed 180 pounds, and after sewing they had to be dragged across to a line of bags ready for carting, which meant we had to have strong backs and solid legs. They were loaded onto the trays of trucks, then carted to the railway sidings and stacked in pyramids. Carrying bags up the pyramid was called 'walking the golden stairway'. The bags were then emptied onto grids where the grain was conveyed on elevators to the various levels of the silos.

Sewing three to four hundred bags in a day was a high amount for a single sewer, but working as a family team we would regularly sew more than that.

The bags were almost as tall as Eddie. Although three years my junior and slightly built, he was as tough as nails. He was given the jobs of bag filler and bag rammer, using a funnel to top them up and a mattock handle to ram them tight before they were sewn.

At age thirteen I was quite stockily built: short but solid, with big thighs. Even my stepfather acknowledged that I was very strong for my age. This meant that when our family was sewing bags together, I was the ideal candidate for dragging them. For a slightly built woman like my mother, and my younger brother Eddie and sister Jeannie, it was an impossible task, meaning that I did most of the bag-shifting. But even for a young teenager this was no mean feat, yet my stepfather saw it as another opportunity for a put-down. 'You've got more brawn than brains,' he said to me. It backfired, though—I took it as a compliment. At least I had something going for me!

~

Heckle had accompanied me to Wycheproof and was often perched on my beret as I walked around, so I was still proudly known as the Birdman. Although I wasn't religious, I saw birds, beginning with the sparrowhawk, as being sort of spiritual. I believed that somehow or other they were sent to me as guardians and protectors as well as companions.

Kookaburras were definitely in that category. I came to learn a lot from them and about them. To begin with, like most other people I thought they were the happiest birds in the world. Then I discovered that their raucous laugh was actually a territorial cry warning other birds, including their own kind, not to encroach on their area—you do so at your peril! That they were monogamous was impressive to me. But above all they appealed to me as great defenders. Wherever I went, they seemed to be watching over me like angels. I begged, borrowed and stole raw mincemeat to feed them, because I liked them instinctively. They liked me for an obvious reason: I was their meal ticket.

It was not uncommon for our family to encounter snakes around the place. We would deliberately make a loud noise when approaching long grass or a hollow log where they were prone to be on warm days, giving them time to slither out of our way. One warm day, a gentle breeze was blowing as Mum hung washing on the outside clothesline. As usual, a kookaburra was in the old gum tree to one side. It seemed he wanted to ensure that every item of clothing was safely hung, as he scanned with his eyes and sharp beak along the line. Mum was occasionally acknowledging his presence, saying, 'Hello, Kooka'. She then turned to me and said, 'Willie, get Kooka some meat.'

I was just about to obey when there was a swish of wings and a loud click of a flashing beak. Kooka had dived like greased lightning and snapped up a snake that had stealthily slithered out of a hole near my feet. Locking his beak around its neck, Kooka flew swiftly up to his branch and beat the snake to death on it.

Mum and I were transfixed, and very thankful. The snake's hole was close to Mum—had she moved one more step along the clothesline, she would have stepped on it and likely been bitten. She turned to me and said, 'I told you, Willie, kookaburras look after you.' She seemed unshaken, as if incidents like that were commonplace. As tough as I thought I was, I couldn't say I was unshaken!

~

Having been surrounded by trees from an early age, it was natural that I should be attracted to them. The majestic gun-barrel straight hardwood trees in the Yarra Valley had first lured me to tree climbing, then to birds and their nests. I was attracted to the thrill of scaling high and difficult trees. I'd seen photos of the tree fellers of the region in the late nineteenth century, and they were my heroes. They would cut notches or scarves into a tree and then hammer a thick board into the cut, doing that board by board until they reached the top of the tree they wanted to lop. I had a few unsuccessful attempts at climbing trees on boards but soon gave up. It was a skill that escaped me, perhaps just as well. I couldn't cut a notch good enough to secure a board, and for whatever reason I kept using boards that were too thin and narrow. Eddie would watch in horror as I wobbled and fell off the narrow board or it sprang out of the inadequate notch and I came crashing down.

In Wycheproof I was able to climb a great variety of trees in my spare time. There were many common gums along the Avoca River and hundreds of dead trees in the paddocks west of town. I'm not proud of this now, but to me the greatest challenge was to climb those dead trees all the way up to the wedgetail eagle nests that they housed. It seemed like I was an infantryman in a war, scaling a mountain as fighter planes buzzed around me. I'm fortunate that although many eagles circled me threateningly, none touched me. They could easily have ripped me away from the tree and flung me to the ground with talons that would have equalled any grappling hook.

Sadly I managed to remove a fledgling eagle from its nest and take it home to be a pet. My stepfather quite rightly scolded me soundly and ordered me in no uncertain terms to take it back. 'What do you want another bird for anyway? You've got your magpie.'

It was a long trek back to the tall dry tree in the middle of a huge paddock. I knew I couldn't just leave the fledgling at the bottom of the trunk, so I made the precarious climb to the nest. There was no sign of the bird's parents as I placed it back amid the loud screeching and savage gestures of its siblings. When I checked on it later that day, it was on the ground again, bereft of many feathers and quite distressed. It had clearly been rejected, probably because of my scent, and was lucky to be alive.

To my knowledge, at that time there were no wildlife shelters— selfishly, I'm glad there weren't. I had no alternative but to take the fledgling home and rear it, and my stepfather understood that. He actually took some interest in my eagle, suggesting it be named 'Lancaster' after the famous British World War II heavy bomber aircraft, which in turn had been named after the town of Lancaster in the county of Lancashire, Victor's birthplace. The Lancaster aircraft had recently been immortalised in the 1955 film *Dam Busters*, based on the true story of Operation Chastise, which involved the bombing of German dams. I loved the film not just because of childhood romanticism of victory in war, but also because of my Lancaster bomber, my marvellous eagle.

In my mind, Lancaster became the most wonderful weapon in my arsenal, superseding the sparrowhawk of my dreams. This awe-inspiring creature was tangible, and he was mine. He took off slowly like his namesake the bomber, but he landed like a helicopter and hovered like one too when he was looking for prey. On warm sunny days he loved to surf the air currents for pure pleasure; his observational flights for hunting purposes, like the reconnaissance flights of the Lancaster bomber, were put aside for an exhilarating half-hour or so of pure self-indulgence. He would glide like a slalom skier on a downhill run but on a slipstream, then catch an updraft to a central point of cross-currents and create his own Ferris wheel in the sky.

Although I could never get as up close and personal with Lancaster as I was with Heckle, I'm sure he saw me as a father-like provider and protector. He seemed to enjoy flying back to land safely on either my outstretched arm or my mum's. The amazing thing was that as razor sharp and large as his talons were, and as heavy as his body was, he always landed gently and harmlessly.

Due to how well trained Lancaster was, and undoubtably also because of the name's connection to Lancashire, Victor was increasingly acknowledging my way with birds—not to me, however. I overheard him a number of times almost boasting to some of his drinking mates about how 'Billy almost reads birds' minds and gets them to do just about anything he wants them to'. Maybe, just maybe, I was proving my stepfather wrong. Maybe, just maybe, I wasn't all brawn!

4

Camouflaged as a clown

The story is told of a man who had been depressed for a long time and finally went to see a psychiatrist. At the end of their session, the psychiatrist said to him, 'I don't think you're clinically depressed. What would perhaps really help you is a good belly laugh. There's a circus in town at the moment, and I'm told they have a terrific clown who has everyone in hysterics. Why don't you go along and see if his humour can lift you out of the doldrums?' Looking seriously at the psychiatrist, the patient said, 'I am that clown!'

Home life was much the same in Wycheproof as it had been in Millgrove. There were always parties on weekends with alcohol flowing freely, and with the alcohol came the violence. I hated this lifestyle. The only upside for me was that the lack of supervision allowed me to act the clown and play pranks. But one prank backfired very badly.

There they were, as drunk as skunks, lying on the couch in the farmhouse, both snoring their heads off in a drunken stupor—my stepfather and his drinking mate Ivan. Ivan's ear was as exposed as a large funnel at the top of a jerry can. Grabbing a glass that held some leftover beer, I poured it into his ear so quickly that it overflowed and dribbled down his neck. I scampered to the kitchen and peered out of the doorway to see what would happen next.

Ivan jerked his head up, looked at my stepfather and roared, 'You bastard!' As though he had instantly sobered up, he sprang at Victor like a jack-in-the-box.

My stepfather, aroused from his drunken sleep by the crazed roar, sat up, heavy eyed and unfocused. Too late—Ivan's fist smashed into his half-open mouth. Blood spurted out, and broken dentures fell like confetti.

To Ivan's amazement, Victor just leapt up and stormed off to his bedroom. But then he suddenly reappeared with glazed eyes and a shotgun pressed to his shoulder, cartridge in place and hammer cocked.

Ivan took off like a bat out of hell, his adrenalin acting like rocket fuel as he raced out the back door and into the paddock. My lasting nightmarish vision is of him running frantically for grim life with my stepfather chasing after him with the shotgun.

~

Another memorable prank, but a much less serious one, was carried out against the local policeman. He was an authority figure like my schoolteachers, so I think it gave me great satisfaction to get back at them through him. But at the time I just knew that the exploit would give me a big rush.

New Year's Eve provided the ideal opportunity. The festivities were in full swing at 11 p.m. when Eddie and I snuck away from our family, who were seated on logs around a camp fire outside Powder-Monkey Jimmy's caravan on the edge of Mount Wycheproof.

Powder-Monkey Jimmy was the explosives man for the quarry on the eastern side of the township. He had been a strong man in a circus and became a significant mentor in my life. He took me under his wing, and while my parents and others were drinking, he concentrated on teaching me gymnastics and other physical and mental exercises. He ingrained some powerful sayings into me, such as 'Our seeming deficits are our greatest assets', and 'You are no one's superior but anyone's equal'. One exercise he taught me was 'backwards jumping', which involved simply jumping backwards from a standing start at a designated line. Each time I jumped he encouraged me to better my previous distance. I was soon out-jumping anyone of my age and many adults as well. His life lesson from this was that 'We often go backwards in life, and when we do, we need extra confidence to know that we can come back and exceed our personal best again'.

A number of hurricane lanterns lit up the area. New Year's celebrations for Powder-Monkey Jimmy and my family, like those for most Australians, consisted mainly of drinking alcohol. In the case of my family, it was a backwoods-style drinking of some very potent moonshine. My stepfather made blackberry wine powerful enough to nearly blow your head off. While the wine was fermenting in its oak barrel, visitors would pour all sorts of spirits into it—whisky, rum and gin, and who knows what else. I shudder to think what percentage of alcohol was in there. This surely accounted for a lot of the violence and sickness that occurred, and it's a wonder some of the drinkers didn't die.

After Eddie and I had crept away from the camp site, we headed for the police station. It backed onto the Anglican church, which backed onto the primary school. We were very familiar with both backyards, having observed them many times at school while retrieving the balls that were often accidentally kicked or thrown over the church fence. We had noticed the little brown Jersey cow in the paddock behind the police station, as well as the small shed where she was milked and sheltered. We knew that the lead rope was always hanging on the open side of the shed.

My brother and I walked up the street and over the hill from Powder-Monkey Jimmy's caravan towards the school. We were carrying whitewash made from slate, lime and chalk. The mix came in packets, so we'd simply added water to the right thickness and stirred. We'd put it in a gallon container and hidden it in our parents' vehicle before going to the party. The walk to our destination was nerve-racking, as though we were carrying a gallon of petrol to use in Molotov cocktails. Eddie seemed especially nervous, hanging behind so much that I had to keep hurrying him along. The closer we got to our destination, the faster we walked. I wanted to get the deed over and done with.

There was a full moon—perhaps that helps explain why we were acting with such lunacy. The moonlight was both good and bad for us: good when we could see where we needed to go, and bad when it seemed to shine on us like a police spotlight.

We were soon heading past the primary school and the church to the rear of the police station. The moon intermittently came out of the clouds, allowing us to locate the cow and leg-rope her to a post behind the shed. She was amazingly compliant, an attitude aided by the bag of fresh lucerne hay we had purloined from a paddock near the school and hidden for this occasion. However, the cow was no longer as cooperative when we started to brush whitewash over her back, jumping and jerking so hard it sounded like the shed was being pulled apart. Surely the noise would be heard by everyone in the house!

We thought our worst fears were confirmed when the back door opened. There was a lot of noise in the house, revealing that the policeman and his family were enjoying their New Year's celebrations at home. My heart skipped a beat, and I momentarily froze. Eddie swore. 'Let's go quietly,' I whispered.

We scampered over the back fence and ducked down. The opening of the outside toilet door allayed our fears, but we still waited with bated breath, concerned that the person might come down to investigate the noise. To our relief, they just went back into the house.

Although we had to stop periodically to let our canvas settle down, we were able to complete our work of art. Apparently the policeman and his family were making such a racket that they could hardly hear anything going on out the back.

On New Year's Day, the whitewashing of the policeman's cow was the talk of the town. Eddie and I grinned at each other knowingly every time we heard about it, and we were very pleased with ourselves. The policeman asked a lot of questions but never managed to track us down.

~

Those were the days of outdoor pit toilets, which consisted of a fairly deep hole or trench with a hut and seat over it. Ours was about six foot deep and three foot wide.

Eddie, Jeannie and I each had a pet lamb, and one day a cry went up. 'There's a lamb down the toilet!'

Eddie and Jeannie went running towards the outhouse with me in their wake. 'Hurry, Eddie!' I shouted. 'I think it's your lamb.'

'How do you know?' Eddie and Jeannie replied in unison.

'I saw it running this way, and mine and Jeannie's weren't with it. Get it quickly, it might drown!'

The three of us were soon peering into the pit, and the smell and the sight were terrible. A creature covered in excrement and urine was standing on its hind legs and bleating pitifully, desperately trying to keep its head above the sewage. It looked more like a large rabbit than a lamb.

I turned to Eddie. 'You'll have to get in there and grab it, or it will die.'

'Why?'

'Because it's your lamb.'

'Yuck! Alright, then. If you're sure it's my lamb . . .'

Modesty demanded that he couldn't strip to his briefs in front of his sister, so he went in fully dressed. With the toilet seat lifted out of the way, he gripped the side of the pit for grim life and slid down gingerly, his face contorted by a grimace.

'How deep is it?' he asked as he reached the bottom.

'Not very deep,' I said. That was if you were six foot tall.

The sewage was quickly over his ankles and well up his legs. 'I can't stand it between my toes!'

The lamb had disappeared, so Eddie fished around in the sludge. Suddenly its head bobbed up.

'Grab it, Eddie!'

He bent over again and nearly fell headfirst into the pit as he made a grab for the lamb. It slipped out of his grasp, thrashing frantically. Jeannie and I gasped as Eddie plunged his arms into the awful concoction again. We glanced at each other and grimaced— double yuck! Then Eddie had the lamb clutched to his chest. The poor animal was in 'it' up to its nostrils. Sewage was in its ears and eyes and all over its face.

Eddie held up the lamb and yelled, 'Grab it!'

'What?' Jeannie and I echoed. 'Throw it up.'

He obeyed. The lamb landed on the ground upright but didn't move. It was standing rigidly, dripping, probably in shock.

Eddie climbed out.

'Well done,' we said.

'Yeah!' he replied in disgust.

The lamb slowly took a couple of steps, and I condescended to put my hands on it and move it on. 'Jeannie, get a bucket of water for us to throw over the lamb,' I said.

'What about me?' Eddie exclaimed.

'Go down to the dam and get clean,' I advised, and he did.

While he was gone, an amazing transformation took place. As the lamb was washed, lo and behold it transpired that this was my lamb.

Jeannie stated the obvious. 'Billy, it's your lamb!'

'So it is,' I said sheepishly.

Eddie was not impressed, to say the least, and neither should he have been. And although he would never normally dob on me to his father because of the repercussions, this time I'd gone too far. I paid the usual price of missing a meal and getting a good hiding. I didn't resist much, though, perhaps a subconscious admission of guilt!

~

The year of the Melbourne Olympics, 1956, our family shifted closer to Wycheproof, on the east side. The property was owned by Tony Lomara, who also owned a cafe in town. Victor was to manage a dairy farm and supervise the hand milking of about a hundred cows day and night. It was another big job shared by a number of members of our family. It was also a fresh chance for me to prove my work ethic—and to pull pranks.

There is an art to successful hand milking. It also involves psychology. The calmer the milker the calmer the cow, and the greater the flow and volume. I observed many times what happened when milkers were bad-tempered or in a foul mood: the cows would respond by shuffling around, kicking if their legs weren't roped back, and withholding some or all of their milk. Even if the milker was calm, cows being milked for the first time often did not take kindly to the idea. The withholding of milk was considered quite serious, not just from a productivity perspective but also for the health of the cow. We were taught that failure to adequately empty an udder could cause the potentially fatal disorder of mastitis, a major problem for the dairy industry because it lowered the quality and quantity of milk. It's now known that mastitis is an infection that is brought about by bacteria or injury and can be prevented with good sanitation.

One of the most distasteful aspects of milking was being swished in the face by tails as the cows flicked them at flies. More often than not, they were soaked in urine and faeces. Being a born prankster, I couldn't help seeing an opportunity for mischief, and my step-brother Tom was my victim.

Tom was a gentle-natured person, but cows tended to be unset-tled when he milked them, perhaps because he was nervous. They would kick him, knock buckets of milk over, and incessantly flick their tails in his face. He was partly to blame for the kicking, because he didn't believe in using a leg rope. I was mainly to blame, however, because many times I would be cunningly talking away to Tom while tickling the cow near the tail, causing it to flick its tail and then get annoyed enough to kick.

Tom was ultimately banned from milking because he couldn't control the cows and get much milk out of them. I thought it was hilarious, but the joke was on me because I had to do much more milking to make up for his absence. While playing the clown continued to be a great relief valve for me, deep down there was a very serious side. I was quite work-oriented and was driven to be the best I could be at whatever I did. 'Son, if you are the best worker in your field,' Powder-Monkey Jimmy had said to me, 'you won't have to apply for jobs—you'll be sought after.' Although that rang true, the real reason that I was so driven with my work at this point was to prove my stepfather wrong. To prove

I had both brains and brawn. That's why I couldn't wait to leave school and work full-time, and more than likely why I worked at the family business for the first two years after I left school.

5

Moving on

I don't remember much of my first formal job. It was 1958, I was fifteen, and I worked as an assistant to the Wycheproof Shire Council engineer. But there was one unforgettable incident at work. I was given the task of dosing the town swimming pool with chlorine, and during my lunchbreak I went for a swim, seemingly too soon. I was quite sick with respiratory problems, and I had nightmares of being overcome by fumes and gasping for breath when I came out of the water. Fortunately the after-effects didn't stay with me.

After I spent a year working for the Wycheproof council, Tony Lomara asked me if I would drove some cattle and sheep for him on weekdays. There was a drought, and grass in the paddocks was very scarce, so the stock needed to find feed along the roadside. I took up the job, which ended up being formative for my Aussie ingenuity and creativity. I was on the road for about a year, and

I had to grow up very quickly. I never really had normal teenage years—I jumped from childhood to adulthood.

For me, droving meant staying with and looking after the sheep and cattle while they grazed during the day, then putting them back into their paddocks at night. The cattle were the dairy cows that our family had been milking, plus a few others, so I was very familiar with them. There were about a hundred cows and approximately fifty ewes. The cows had to be back at the shed each night in time to be milked and were not taken back out on the road until after milking the next day. Droving sheep and cattle together wasn't easy; they were such different animals that had it not been for my dog Rusty's ability to round up anything that moved, they would have been unmanageable.

The job suited my solitary nature at that age, and I wasn't entirely without company. Farmers and their wives would drive past and sometimes stop to have a chat. Rusty, a very keen kelpie, was with me as my constant companion. I could confide in him about anything, and he never disagreed with me or criticised me or argued with me! He just accepted me as I was, and licked and loved me nearly to death, sitting at my feet and gazing up at me with adoring eyes.

Rusty was the real drover, and I his assistant. He was brilliant at his job—fast and alert and tough and very intelligent. He instinctively knew when a cow or ewe was wandering away. As quick as a flash he would head it off, not by rushing at it but by slowly pacing a wide circle in front of it and making his commanding presence known. He had an authoritative bark and would brush against the sides of their legs as if he was going to nip them.

The animals soon got the message that they couldn't get away from him.

In those days there was no way to call for help if anything went wrong. You had to be a rescue worker for sheep or cattle that got stuck in riverbeds or roadside dams, a veterinarian to help them give birth, and a surgeon to stitch them up when they cut themselves on barbed-wire fencing. I had to turn quite a few lambs and calves around to prevent a breech birth, and I stitched up a number of wounds using a large but ordinary sewing needle and a gut fishing line—it did the trick, and the stitches dissolved in time.

Rusty was an amazing hero on one occasion. He and I were droving alongside the Avoca River when the water was so low that it had stopped running. The river was little more than waterholes, which were drying up and diminishing day by day. It wasn't easy for me to find enough for the stock and also keep them from rushing into the middle of the river, where the quicksand-like mud was deep enough that they could get bogged. I had to be as sharp as a hawk. I searched for the largest bodies of water and engaged Rusty to keep the stock moving towards those spots, while we bypassed smaller waterholes. Without Rusty it would have been impossible.

All his attributes were put to the test on this particular day. As we approached the river, the cattle were very thirsty and surged forward as one, at breakneck speed. 'Way back!' I shouted to Rusty, the signal to head them off and round them up. He didn't need a second command.

I raced ahead on my bike to survey the scene. The mob had been heading for a low-lying pool surrounded by lots of mud.

Some cattle had managed to reach the bank before Rusty drove them back onto the roadside, where he was circling them like a shark with a shoal of fish. I glanced along the river in the hope of sighting a deeper waterhole. As I did, I noticed a cow stuck in the mud near where the herd had been.

She was frantically thrashing around and sinking deeper. I hurried over to assess the situation. At first it looked too risky for me to get alongside it, then I spotted a half-submerged tree trunk near the cow. I stood on it and tried to move her, but the more I touched her the more she struggled and sank further into the mud. I was exhausted from holding her head up out of the mud and was reluctantly about to let her go.

Then I heard Rusty barking incessantly, too loud and constant to be aimed just at cattle.

To my amazement and relief, Rusty and a nearby farmer, Stan Boyd, appeared over the riverbank. 'Got a bit of a problem have you, Bill?'

'You could say that.'

'What do you need?'

'Aspros, I think!'

'Nah, I'll have to pull her out with a tractor.'

'I think you're right.'

'Say no more. My brother is over the bank holding the cattle with his dog. I'll hold the cattle and send him to get our tractor. Can you hang on there?'

'Yes. With help on the way I've got a new lease of life!'

Although it seemed like an eternity, it wasn't long before Stan's brother returned and pulled the cow out. Then the farmers told me of the remarkable way that Rusty had got their attention. They'd been driving past when they recognised the kelpie and the mob of cattle, and they'd wondered why I wasn't there. As they drove closer, Rusty suddenly left the mob and ran towards their ute, barking loudly. He ran right onto the road, so it was just as well there were no other vehicles coming the other way. Stan and his brother pulled to a stop, and Rusty ran up to the driver's side door, still barking frantically. When Stan got out, Rusty led him right over to me. What a hero!

~

While droving I met the district's last swagman, Fred Blamey. On one occasion, as he was walking along the road with his heavy swag on his back, a farmer drove up to him with his horse and dray. 'Like a ride, Fred?'

Fred nodded, then struggled under his load as he climbed up alongside the farmer.

When they started to move along, the farmer said to Fred, 'Why don't you take that great swag off your back?'

Fred replied laconically, 'I thought it might be too heavy for the horses!'

In his final days on the road, Fred dispensed with his swag and would carry two suitcases. However, he didn't carry them together—he would carry one suitcase ahead a hundred yards or so, then go back for the second suitcase and repeat the process along the road.

Fred finally retired to live with his daughter and son-in-law in town. I can still picture him in his nineties, a rope over his shoulder, dragging logs to cut up for firewood. Passers-by used to laugh at Fred, but he would just drawl back, 'Every step adds a minute to my life.' Not a bad philosophy.

~

After my year of droving, I accepted a job offer from a local share-farmer, Gus. I'd been working with him for a while when I had quite a testing experience.

Gus share-farmed a remote property that needed to be culti-vated, and I was allocated the task of going up and cultivating it. He brought drums of fuel to the property, while I drove the tractor and scarifier there. I was to sleep in an old stable, and Gus dropped off some blankets and a pillow along with the fuel. He told me he would bring food supplies later that day. I had a sandwich lunch and carried plenty of water in a hessian bag on the tractor, some-thing all farmers kept on their vehicles in those days. To replenish it, there was a dam on the property with pretty clean water.

Gus still hadn't turned up by dinnertime. Although I was hungry I convinced myself that there was some simple explanation for him being delayed so long, and that he would arrive later. I kept driving the tractor into the night, looking hopefully at every set of headlights that appeared on the adjacent road. They all went past. Tiredness ultimately overcame me, so I drove back to the stable and lay down exhausted. I went to sleep immediately, oblivious to any mice, rats, snakes or other creatures that may have been running around during the night.

I woke up early, cold and hungry, and a few gulps of water only made me feel colder. So I started a fire. Watching the flames dance around didn't make me think of ballet—it made me think of one of my favourite dishes, curried stew.

Why on earth hasn't Gus turned up? I wondered. His wife was a caring woman, and I would have thought she was in the loop of what was happening. Surely over their own dinner she'd asked him what my arrangements were, then told him in no uncertain terms to bring me the supplies or even brought them herself.

It was no good sitting around thinking—I was getting hungrier by the minute. At least the magpies were happy, warbling away to welcome the dawn. The kookaburras seemed to think my situation was funny. Lots of brown sparrows were flying and hopping around the stables expectantly, like they would in sowing time with lots of seed on the ground. The crows were cawing like a back-up group to the magpie choir. As enticing as the fire was, my hunger was stronger, so I had to get moving and distract myself. Gus would soon be there, and then I'd have all the missed meals in one. I fuelled up the tractor and went back to work.

By midmorning there was still no sign of Gus. Suddenly, as the dust swirled around the tractor cabin, I had a vision, clear as crystal. It consisted of three whole bricks, a half brick, a stick and some wheat. An ingenious Aussie invention had been born: a sparrow trap. Roast sparrows would soon be on the menu!

I drove the tractor to the stable, found the bricks I needed and scooped some wheat from a drum. Then I set the trap: I lay the two bricks on the ground on their edge, parallel to each other; then placed the half brick between their ends, to set them apart and form a U-shape; I balanced the third brick in between them on its flat side, propped up by a light stick to act as a trapdoor;

and wheat sprinkled inside. My idea was that sparrows would flock in to eat the wheat, they would bump the stick, and then the brick balanced on the stick would fall and hey presto, sparrows for lunch!

I got back on the tractor and cultivated a few more rounds of the paddock. With every round, I visualised my trap packed with succulent sparrows. I also imagined writing about it for a book on Aussie survival tips.

After about an hour I drove the tractor over to the shed and checked the trap. The trapdoor was still up, and all the wheat gone. Darn it—the stick was too thick. I experimented a bit and got a stick barely able to hold the weight of the brick trapdoor. This time when I put some wheat in the trap, I put some grains outside as well. If enough excited sparrows followed the trail inside the trap and fluttered their wings sufficiently, the stick would trip and the trapdoor fall with them inside.

I got on the tractor, did some more laps of the paddock and went back in. This time the trap had been sprung. As I drew closer I could hear loud chirping from inside, but then I realised something: how could I lift the lid off the trap without the sparrows escaping? Necessity is the mother of invention—there was a hessian sugar bag in the tractor toolbox.

I slid the open end under all the bricks and jerked it up, encasing everything. Sparrows were fluttering frantically in the bag. I killed and plucked the four of them, then used a piece of fencing wire for a fork as I chargrilled them in the fire. They were delicious, or was that only because I was starving hungry and anything would have tasted nice, even old boot leather?

There were only a couple of tablespoons of meat per bird, so during the course of the day I caught another ten or twelve. I had gourmet sparrow for lunch and afternoon tea, and was as full as a goog and doubly satisfied that I was not only a successful hunter but an ideas man as well. Thanks to the sparrows, I lived off the land for three days. The experience gave me increased confidence in my ability to survive.

I never found out what had happened to Gus. When I drove the tractor and scarifier back, mission accomplished, he was very apologetic, and his wife even more so, but there was no explanation.

～

During my time working with Gus, he was often visited by one of his old schoolmates, another local farmer named Des Wood, with whom he had remained close friends. Des would come by to see how things were going and help to repair broken implements. He would also attend social gatherings with Gus and his family. I visited the Woods' farm, just outside Wycheproof, whenever Gus sought advice from Des or his father Charlie on some farming matter or wanted to borrow a piece of their machinery.

Des and Charlie got to know me and my work very well, and vice versa. Not long after the abandonment incident, Des offered me a live-in job on his farm. He said he'd discussed it with his father, who was keen to have me on board. Des also consulted with his old friend. Although Gus was reluctant to let me go, he was struggling financially and could barely afford to keep me on. It was a wrench to leave Gus and his family, with whom I'd become very close, but I accepted the offer.

6

A glimmer of light

Charlie Wood was an incredibly kind and compassionate man. He had served in World War I, not as an infantryman but as a stretcher-bearer. His courage and loyalty were never doubted as he stretchered out the wounded from the thick of battle.

Charlie had a schoolmate, Albert Nioa, who enlisted and trained with him. After the hell of Anzac Cove started, they were separated and thrown into the fray as thousands of men charged at each other with bayonets, grenades and guns. Albert was bearing arms, and Charlie was on the end of a stretcher. Amid a terrible cacophony of bombs and artillery fire and shouts and screams, Charlie and a fellow stretcher-bearer rushed out to rescue the wounded and take them to a makeshift field hospital. The two men were gently but urgently placing a badly wounded soldier on the stretcher, when to Charlie's horror and great surprise he recognised that it was Albert. What were the odds? He survived but lost his leg and was repatriated home.

After the war, Albert and his brother Danny bought soldier settlement blocks next to Charlie's. Albert and Charlie were Anzac blood brothers, which meant Albert was as close to Charlie as Danny, or even closer in some respects. That baptism by fire at Gallipoli had been like a marriage ceremony for them, making the two one in spirit—till death they would not part. As next-door neighbours, Charlie, Albert and Danny shared every major farming task imaginable: harvesting crops, shearing, crutching and drenching sheep, fencing, and cutting wood. Charlie had two children with his first wife before her death and then got remarried to a woman a few years younger than him.

Albert was a prankster. Like me, he used humour as a distraction and to help him get through hard times. I well remember him pulling a prank on me not long after I started working for the Woods, when I was helping them drench their sheep. Albert and I were putting the animals into a pen through long grass, when all of a sudden he cried out, '*Aarggh, a snake! It's bitten me!*'

I rushed over to him anxiously as he was rolling up his trousers.

'Got you!' he exclaimed, revealing his wooden leg.

He had got me all right, well and truly.

Albert never believed that the loss of his leg was a disability. He fulfilled one of my mentor's saying that day: 'Our seeming deficits are our greatest assets'.

Charlie took me under his wing. He was like the father I never knew, and a teacher as well.

Although television had just become available in Australia, the Woods didn't have a set; evenings were used instead for recreational and motivational purposes. Charlie introduced me to the game of draughts, which we would play each evening after dinner while he gave me life lessons that corresponded with our moves. 'Think ahead.' 'Look before you leap.' 'Be thoughtful and strategic about the moves you make in life, and then be definite and decisive and swift when you do make a move.' Charlie instilled these ideas and many more in me. They have stayed with me and stood me in good stead over my lifetime.

I'd started working for the Woods just before seed-sowing time in winter, when we needed to sow crops of wheat, barley and oats. Although I was already an experienced tractor driver, Charlie helped me to improve my skills. 'Driving is not just about driving,' he would say. 'It's about being ever alert while being in tune with your vehicle and your environment.' He was teaching me to think ahead, to look ahead, to look back and to look around; to listen for any irregularities, and to care for the vehicle and the machinery. 'Prevention is better than cure, as far as time and cost are concerned. Always check the water and oil levels in the motor, and the air pressure in the tyres. Be aware of obstacles like the jagged tops of tree stumps, barely above the ground, that can tear a tyre irreparably.' Charlie applied similar instructions to our bodies and to life in general. 'Look after your body like you would machinery that you don't want to break down. Eat well, drink well, sleep well. Get plenty of exercise and ideally play a sport.'

He was gentle with me during our games of draughts, although he always won. At times he was clearly allowing me to be almost even with him, then coming up and beating me to teach me yet another lesson. 'You can be so near and yet so far from achieving your goals in life. You need to follow through and finish off, and spare no effort in doing so.' I watched Charlie very closely as he found ways to block my advancement. He varied his play sometimes so that I couldn't easily anticipate his moves, and he would think two or three moves ahead and lay traps for me. He encouraged me throughout, however. 'You've got a good head on your shoulders, Bill. You're improving. You're starting to stretch me.'

After a couple of weeks I finally won a game—or I think I did. You never really knew with Charlie. He was so accomplished at making me feel good and boosting my self-confidence that I've never been sure if letting me win was part of his plan. On the other hand he was such a sincere and honest man that I suspect when he said I had won on my own merit, I probably had.

~

All of a sudden, my world shattered. Charlie died of a massive stroke only about three months after he and Des had given me the opportunity of a lifetime. No one had suspected that the constant indigestion he thought he was suffering was something much more serious—the copious quantities of indigestion tablets he was taking were camouflaging a major heart problem.

Charlie had shown me the power of mentoring someone, even if only briefly. He left no stone unturned in his desire to assist me in life. Even when he was gravely ill in hospital, he was still thinking of me, giving instructions to his wife and son to look after me should anything happen to him. On the day of his funeral, when I was shocked and distraught, and Mrs Wood heartbroken, I remember her saying to me, 'Don't worry, we'll look after you. That's what Charlie wanted.' And look after me they did. Des treated me more like a brother than an employee, and Mrs Wood treated me like a son.

I'd known Charlie for a relatively short period of time, yet he'd had an enormous impact on me. There was something quite different about him. I knew he was very spiritual and a devout churchgoer, but he didn't preach it—he lived it. He had strong convictions and carried them out. He wasn't a conscientious objector to war, but he was personally opposed to killing, which was why he'd chosen to be a stretcher-bearer and not an arms-bearer. No one could ever doubt his courage or his devotion to King and Country.

In the midst of my grief I couldn't get around what I had witnessed and experienced through being in Charlie's life. He had reminded me of my kind teacher Mr Godfrey and the business owner who had caught me shoplifting, except I'd spent much more time with Charlie, absorbing his love, his understanding, and his interest in my welfare. For a fleeting moment, I wondered if there could be a God like the one my mother believed in. But what about everything that had happened and was still happening to me and my family?

Albert was shattered when Charlie died. As tough and hardened as he was, he was inconsolable. His schoolmate, blood brother, and lifelong friend and neighbour—the hero who had saved his life— had gone without warning, without saying goodbye. Only Charlie's immediate family had been able to see him in hospital before he died. But even if Albert had been given the chance, he probably wouldn't have visited his old friend straight away. In his mind there was nothing major wrong with Charlie, who wouldn't be staying in hospital; he was bulletproof, indestructible, godlike. Albert was never the same again. A part of him was missing—the spark in his life, Charlie.

~

Des continued his dad's great partnership and comradeship with the Nioa brothers after Charlie's death. They had also built up a close working relationship with their neighbours the Boyd brothers, Stan and Billy. That year the Woods, Nioas and Boyds worked together for three weeks to shear their sheep. Billy and Des were the shearers, and Stan and I were the rouseabouts in the shed, picking up, throwing and baling the fleeces while keeping the floor around the shearers clear. Albert and Danny looked after the sheep outside, branding them as they were shorn and then transferring them back to their paddocks. We didn't shear on Saturdays and certainly not on Sundays, as Des was a devout churchgoer.

He was also a very keen sportsman who played football and cricket on Saturdays in season, as well as some golf. After acquiring a pilot's licence, he flew regularly. He encouraged me to get involved in sport too, and I played footy on Saturdays and cycled competitively on Sundays.

Des encouraged me enormously. He had great faith in my farming abilities and trusted me to do the job, whether it was driving a tractor or truck, throwing or shearing a fleece, or blocking firewood. If the task was new to me, he would simply demonstrate it and then leave me alone to work it out; he never looked over my shoulder to supervise me. It was as if he'd read my mind. I didn't like people looking over my shoulder when I was doing something; it made me more nervous by the minute, to the point where I was likely to muck up the task. Whenever I'd worked for my stepfather, he had constantly looked over my shoulder and criticised me.

Sometimes, however, I was dangerously overconfident when I worked for Des. I vividly remember the first time I drove one of his tractors at sowing time. He was watching me as I headed off with the tractor and combine to sow the first lap of a large paddock. About a hundred yards ahead, just out from the fence line, was a big dead tree. The space between it and the fence was barely wider than the combine. I should have noticed that this area had not been cultivated, but my overconfidence blinded me. Without batting an eyelid I drove the tractor pulling the combine through the gap, just brushing against the tree. I was shocked when I realised how narrowly I'd got through and how careless I had been with Des's equipment. I looked back to see him wiping his forehead as a gesture of relief and probably disbelief.

True to Des's amazingly tolerant attitude towards me, he never raised the incident again. I hope I learnt from it.

7

Payback

Although I was working away from home from the age of fifteen until I got a live-in job, I still went home weeknights and weekends.

My home, for as long as I could remember, had been a place of alcohol abuse, violence, and associated sordidness. There were constant brutal fights, and not just between men. My mother was frequently beaten by my stepfather and one of my stepbrothers. All sorts of dubious characters hung out at our house, coming and going as they pleased. The lure was not just alcohol, but my six beautiful sisters.

I despaired at not being able to protect my mother and sisters, and I tried to brighten up their lives in the midst of such a dark place. Eddie did the same. On nights when the family home became a house of horrors, he would take the girls into hiding and give them sweets he'd bought with the money from plucking sheep and bag sewing. I endeavoured to get the girls away from the house as much as I could. I'd take them on outings, putting Norma on the handlebars and Gladys on the frame of my trusty old Malvern Star pushbike. I gave them treats too, and for one of Gladys's birthdays I rode through floodwaters to bring her a Noddy book and a doll.

Weekends were when hell happened—they were one drunken, debauched party. The most undesirable males would hang around harassing my sisters.

A farmer with an ugly reputation was having a drinking session at our home again and making sexual overtures in his loud conversations. Mum called it 'just boy's talk', although his hands were roaming like an octopus's tentacles over the women present. He was also throwing his weight around, challenging everyone to arm wrestles and sparring matches.

I could see what he was about and believed that if I could defeat him it would send a message that he'd better back off. 'I'll take you on,' I said resolutely, as I walked quickly and nervously towards him. 'I'll wrist wrestle you.'

He laughed at me and said sarcastically, 'Do your best, son.' When we locked fingers, he forced mine back so savagely that he nearly broke my wrist. He then pushed me away like he was brushing off a fly.

It was then I realised how powerless I was to protect myself, let alone anyone else. I went outside into the dark and cried my eyes out. I hated him. I wanted to kill him. My stepfather kept a shotgun and ammunition in the house, so it wouldn't have been hard.

When Mum came to check on me, I angrily made my thoughts known. Her reasoning averted disaster. 'Who wins if you do that,

Billy? He will be gone, but so will you—in prison for a long time. You won't be around to protect us.'

~

One of the most important things the Woods encouraged me to do was to arrange to have a new prosthetic eye made and fitted. 'You're handsome enough now, Bill, but how much more handsome you'd be with a new eye,' Mrs Woods would say.

I was seventeen, and had been walking around with an empty eye socket for about twelve years. It took me a while to save for it. There was no government assistance in those days. I had one made and fitted at the Royal Victorian Eye and Ear Hospital in Melbourne. Because I had not had an eye for so long my eye socket had closed considerably and a number of increasingly large eyes had to be made and squeezed tightly in to force the surrounding muscles wide enough to fit the correct size eye again. A painful process. It necessitated travelling by train some three hundred and forty-four miles to Melbourne, roundtrip, a number of times. Eddie went with me.

It was around this time that a heightened awareness of my physical and sexual abuse was tormenting me. Not infrequently, suicidal and murderous thoughts came into my mind. My physical salvation came in the form of a local policeman, Senior Constable Frank Mannix, and the Wycheproof Police and Citizens Youth Club that he headed up.

Constable Mannix was a typical country cop of that era. He had a wife and six children, and he worked hard at establishing a rapport with the farming community, particularly its youth, so that law and order would be understood and respected. As an example of his practical engagement with the community, he took locals for their driving tests, including me when I turned eighteen.

Des had asked me if I'd be interested in buying Charlie's car. Like many women of her era, Mrs Wood had never learnt to drive, and she had no intention of learning so late in life. Des felt it would be ideal for me to have my own car to learn in before I got my licence, and so I could drive Mrs Wood around when he wasn't available. The car was a robust 1948 Austin A40 Devon. Charlie had bought it new, and it was in good condition with low miles on the speedo. It was offered to me very cheaply, and I bought it without hesitation.

Come licence test day, Des drove with me to the police station. Constable Mannix was waiting and said to Des, 'I'll take over from here.' He was completely disarming. 'I hear you're burning up the bike circuit at Charlton and playing a pretty good game of footy. In fact, I saw you take a great speccy the other Saturday. How's the old man and your mum? I suppose I'd better get down to tin tacks. Des tells me you're a good little driver. That you've had plenty of practice driving his ute around the paddocks as well as getting used to being on the road. Not on your own, though, I suppose?'

No comment from me.

I passed my test with flying colours, but although I had been thoroughly tested it hadn't seemed like I was being tested much at all. Such was Mannix's ability to put people at ease. He had certainly established a rapport with me.

After he had completed the paperwork for my licence in his office, he sowed a seed in my mind. First he asked me how much I weighed, and I replied, 'Just under 147 pounds, I think.'

'You know, Bill, you'd make a good welterweight boxer. I've been watching you at footy—you've got a really solid build, big thighs, thick arms. And Des tells me you're very strong, lumping bags of wheat. You're also fast on your feet and well balanced. You'd be good in the ring. Why don't you come down to the club on Monday and check it out?'

Des had already told me about the Police and Citizens Youth Club, and I'd meant to check it out, never connecting it with self-defence. Now the penny dropped. I very much wanted to be a good enough boxer to protect Mum and the girls, and to send a strong message to my abusers as well.

The following Monday I went to the club. It was pretty plain, set up in a hall at the back of the shire council building. It had a ping-pong table, a badminton court, weights, exercise equipment, pummel horses for gymnastics and a couple of punching bags and speedballs. There was no dedicated raised boxing ring; evidently a ring was improvised when bouts were scheduled.

After Constable Mannix set me to work on a punching bag and speedball, he had a bit of a spar with me and left it at that for the first session. The following week an improvised ring was waiting, and I was put in it for the first time. 'Let's see what you're made of,' Mannix said. I was tentative and apprehensive until he added, 'Treat me as your worst enemy. Hit me like you hate the sight of me and have plenty to pay back!'

I forgot about being a stylish boxer and became an aggressive fighter who never took a step back, so much so that soon Mannix couldn't handle me in the ring. He got a trainer for me, an experienced boxer who could deal with me.

~

My boxing was to change everything, including the life of my stepbrother Ellis. Sadly, because of all the years he spent separated from his father in a children's home during the second world war, Ellis longed to be with Victor and to please him. When Mum took Ellis into our home after marrying his father, the boy tried desperately to walk in Victor's footsteps. He drank heavily and threw his weight around, often as his father's right hand in acts of domestic violence. Eventually Ellis joined the regular army, but he was soon discharged partly due to his drinking problem.

One weekend, after some months of training for my first fight, I was home during the same-old, same-old Saturday night scene. Dubious characters were present, and an inebriated Ellis was getting more aggressive by the minute. Next moment he made a sarcastic comment, which I didn't hear, about 'one-eyed, weak-as-water Billy who couldn't fight his way out of a brown paper bag'.

Mum objected to Ellis talking about me like that and told him to stop it. He continued in a similar vein until she told him to get out of the house.

'Try and get me out, you bitch,' he shouted.

With that, Mum grabbed him and tried to push him out. He punched into her, knocking her down.

I was outside when one of the girls—Jeannie, I think—came rushing out saying, 'Ellis has knocked Mum down, come quickly!'

I didn't need any urging. I rushed in as Mum was being assisted up. There was no blood, and she appeared all right and said she was. Ellis was still being belligerent, though, especially now that I was present. 'I could take you anytime,' he slurred.

'Really.'

'*Yeah!*' He lurched at me.

Mum was screaming at him, wanting to grab him again, but she was held back.

His arms were flailing so wide open that it looked like he wanted to embrace me. I simply shaped up in front of him, and instead of giving him a sledgehammer straight right to the chin, I gave him a short, sharp direct blow to the jaw like the punch I'd give a speed-ball. That shook him up considerably, but he regained momentum and continued charging at me. I sidestepped him, then gave him a very solid roundarm punch to the stomach. He exhaled like an air mattress being deflated and sank down like a bag of potatoes. He had nothing more to say or do.

Bystanders were saying, 'Serve you right,' and 'Good on you, Billy'.

Following that, Ellis had a different attitude towards me and Mum. He'd obviously realised he couldn't get away with laying a hand on either of us again, and he appeared to be trying to make amends. Together with Eddie he was present and support-ive at all of my fights, becoming one of my biggest fans. Although I was appreciative of his support, I couldn't forgive him for his past behaviour towards Mum and I.

~

The greatest inspiration for my fighting style came from world heavyweight champion Joe Louis. I had read of his title fight against light heavyweight Billy Conn in 1941, considered to be one of the greatest heavyweight fights of all time. Although much lighter than Louis, Conn wouldn't put on weight for the fight. When asked what his tactics would be with such a disadvantage, he said, 'I'll use a run-and-hit strategy. Run him off his feet, then knock him out!' Louis's famous laconic response was, 'He can run but he can't hide!' Louis knocked Conn out with two seconds to go in the thirteenth round. 'He can run but he can't hide' became my own inspiration for my fights.

I won my first two fights by knockouts (KOs). The third fight was to be in my hometown against a local guy about my age who fancied himself a much better boxer than me. Whether this was because of jealousy or snobbery, I'm not sure, but he looked down his nose at me and sneered while watching me train. He talked up his ability in the ring and strutted around town flexing his muscles. He certainly had an impressive physique: broad shoulders, solid pectoral and solar plexus muscles, and a sixpack. Soon he'd talked himself into a corner. 'I could knock Sutcliffe's head off blindfolded.'

'Then put your gloves where your mouth is—get in the ring with Bill!' the old-timers urged. 'Bill will chew you up and spit you out!'

It was all too much for Mr Universe's pride, and he was locked into a bout.

The youth club was packed that night. Most hadn't seen me fight before, and despite my impressive record I'm sure the majority were expecting me to be beaten by the one who looked the part and pranced around impressively.

The starting bell sounded. My opponent and I touched gloves. 'Come out fighting,' the referee ordered.

I did, but my opponent came out prancing like a show pony. He was sparring into the air with his gloves, as though he was doing a light training session, and smiling like a celebrity. *How arrogant,*

I thought. To me he was no longer the town glamour boy but my enemy, representing all the evil abusers in my life.

He was totally on the back foot, dancing around desperately as he tried to avoid my blows. I stalked him mercilessly around the ring like a possessed person. I was an unusual southpaw because of my prosthetic left eye—I was protecting it.

This fight didn't take thirteen rounds. I cornered my evasive opponent about halfway through the first round. His eyes were now full of fear instead of confidence while I kept raining blows on him with a right-left, left-right combination. His nose started bleeding and was running like a tap.

The referee called a temporary halt. My opponent's seconds began cleaning him up and stuffing his nostrils with wadding. I'd barely raised a sweat; I had raised a thirst, though, which was soon quenched by my seconds. 'Let's get on with it,' I said, glancing over at my opponent.

He looked like he was patched up, but there was an animated conversation going on. Then, to my amazement, his handlers were motioning to the referee. He had thrown in the towel! I was declared the winner by a technical knockout (TKO) in the first round. It had been a very easy fight and a very satisfying one.

~

After winning seven fights in a row by KOs and TKOs, I had a fearsome reputation. During the next one, my opponent only managed to evade me for a minute or so before I caught up with him and delivered my lethal combination. Again, I won by TKO.

My next fight was to be an exhibition and testimonial bout for a boxer nearing the end of an illustrious career, and I felt privileged to be boxing with him. But the night before, I had a strange experience.

I was taking a shower when, all of a sudden, emotions started to mount up in me. Despite my considerable progress in life and relative success, I was overwhelmed by the weight of my past experiences. Every drop of water coming out of the showerhead seemed to represent every sordid incident that had occurred in my life. Instead of cascading gently over me, the droplets were hitting me like sledgehammer blows. My head was racked with pain, and my chest was heaving with uncontrollable emotion. Then the tears started to flow, not in relief but in torment. It seemed that they were more numerous than the water drops. I couldn't take it anymore.

'God help me!' I blurted out, not intentionally but spontaneously.

Like in a passing storm, the rain of my emotions suddenly stopped. Thinking nothing more of it, I dried off, put my pyjamas on, went to bed and slept like a log.

The following day, fight day, I pottered around on the farm. In the morning I walked around a paddock, cutting out some Scotch thistles with a mattock, but I kept stopping to think about how I might fare against such an accomplished boxer. That was more tiring than using the mattock, so I had lunch, listened to an episode of the 'Blue Hills' radio series, and had a nap for a couple of hours.

When I woke up I was prompted to kneel and pray. It was a selfish prayer again. I was conscious that even though this was to be an exhibition bout, more than likely there would be talent scouts there because I was an up-and-comer. I asked God to help me perform so well that I might get a good offer from a manager and be able to turn professional. Visions of my previous wins were clear in my mind.

When I got up off my knees, an odd feeling came over me. Instead of feeling confident and exhilarated about my fight as I normally did, I felt quite flat. Was it too much introspection, or depression? I don't know. It presented itself like a fog in my mind.

After an early dinner, I drove over to pick up Eddie and Ellis. On the way to the fight, held in the nearby township of Donald, they sensed something was wrong and asked me if I was feeling all right. Again I couldn't put my finger on what was going on. I was certainly quieter than usual, but it wasn't as if I was mulling in my mind. My mind was blank. They asked me what my opponent was like, and I told them all I knew, which wasn't much—I preferred not to know too much. He was in his thirties and at the end of a good boxing career, a local schoolteacher with more wins than losses under his belt.

When I stepped under the ropes that night, my gloves felt like lead and my legs felt like they had a ball and chain attached to them. Although the fight was supposed to be a swansong for my opponent, it was clear he wasn't about to settle for demonstrating how to throw fancy punches. He was all about trying to teach the relatively new kid on the block a boxing lesson and knock him out. For the first time in my career I was put on the defensive. Instead of being the chaser I was the chased. Not that I ran away—I stood and slugged it out but defensively rather than offensively.

I'd never gone the full distance of a fight before, but I had confidence in my fitness and endurance. My training regime was all about working hard for long periods of time. The trouble was with my mind; it was inexplicably foggy.

Eddie and Ellis were in my corner and kept shouting out, 'Go for him, Bill, take the lead, don't let him keep coming at you.'

And my trainer was roaring out, 'Offensive, offensive, offensive!' He gave the same pep talk at the end of each round. 'What's the matter with you, Bill? You've never ever taken a backwards step, and now you are! Get out there and take it up to him. Offensive, offensive, *offensive!*' Offensive fighting involved constantly forging forward like a bulldozer. It was the only type of fighting I knew, but it had all gone out the window now.

As the bell rang for the last round, my trainer pushed me into the ring. I tried again to take the lead, but all to no avail. There was only a referee adjudicating without judges, because it was supposed to be an exhibition bout, but after our performance he had no alternative but to take the fight seriously and declare a winner. And that winner had to be my opponent, who had undoubtedly accumulated the most points.

He was magnanimous about my defeat, telling me it must have been 'just one of those nights we all have'. But we had a rematch and exactly the same thing happened.

In my brief boxing career I had ten amateur bouts. Five of them I won by KOs and three by TKOs, and two I lost by points to the same opponent. I retired prematurely. Was my pride dented too much? Was I only man enough to take wins and not losses? I don't think so. I had sustained losses in bike races, and it hadn't affected me like this. What was going on? I recalled my prayer before my second-last bout: 'God help me.' Had He? I couldn't see how. All my old doubts about an omniscient God came back. I kept asking, 'Why? Why? Why?' And even if my doubts were trivial to God, they were important for me to become a believer.

8

Itchy feet

My last fight had heralded the beginning of a completely different era for me. I was becoming a very goal-oriented person—not unlike many people, I suppose, who start to find their feet and realise they have gifts and talents and could perhaps be reasonable achievers.

Des recognised that I was driven by a deep desire to be successful in my working life as much as in my sporting life. He came up with a great business idea for me, which he said I could pursue in addition to my work with him. Observing my love of timber and my familiarity with sawmilling, he suggested I supply firewood to businesses and residences in Wycheproof and surrounding townships. His only condition was that I cut and cart the wood in my spare time.

Hundreds of ringbarked dead trees were standing in Des's paddocks, a testament to the tree-clearing frenzy that farmers had gone through post–World War II. Des and his dad had been cutting down some of those trees for over thirty years, and there were still many left. 'More than enough firewood for my lifetime, and lots more as well,' Des told me. 'I know the publicans in Wycheproof and Charlton, and I'm sure they'd be interested in buying firewood at the right price.' When I approached them they were more than happy with my price and delivery timeline, and I soon established a very profitable business.

Des encouraged me to save and invest as much money as I could from my earnings. I was able to afford my prosthetic eye because of the money I saved.

The late 1950s and early 1960s saw the advent of timber plantations as investments in renewable resources, and I joined Des in buying many shares.

An incredibly generous person, Des gave me a bonus each year of at least a hundred-acre paddock. I cultivated, sowed and harvested the land in my own time. He supplied the fuel and fertiliser each year, and the seed for the first year. After that I used my own seed but was still allowed to use all his equipment. It was very lucrative and a great incentive for me to develop business skills.

I'd been a good boxer and was a good farmer, and I was an emerging businessman with the beginning of an investment portfolio. There was a problem, however. In each of these areas I would reach for the stars in wanting to be the best, but that was like chasing a crock of gold at the end of a rainbow. I would follow a dream and get within reach of the crock of gold, but suddenly it would fade into the distance like a mirage and disappear. I would become disillusioned and then follow another dream, but the same thing would happen. Nothing could fulfil or satisfy me.

The Woods encouraged me to go to church. Commendably they didn't try to get me to attend the Catholic church with them, but suggested I go to the Anglican church. It was the nominal church of my stepfather, where he had been christened and married but which he no longer attended. I certainly didn't find rest in God there—reading from their prayerbook, singing from their hymnbook, and consuming Communion wafers and wine did nothing for me. In fact it was beyond my belief.

I'd been oscillating between atheism and agnosticism. At this stage I was veering closer to agnosticism, very experimental— especially so with prayer. I expected that an almighty God would prove His presence and power by granting my every request, mostly selfish ones. It was like a child's attitude to Santa Claus: 'Give me, give me, give me. I want, I want, I want.'

Overall, attending church was a disappointing experience for me. Goodness seemed only to apply on Sundays; for the rest of the week most churchgoers seemed no better than anyone else. Many of my peers who were religious would go to Confession on a Saturday to be forgiven of all their sins, then go and sin their heads off over the weekend and during the week. It was about this time that my mother quoted some religious words to me, the only occasion I remember her doing so. 'Our hearts are restless until they find their rest in God.' These were words from Augustine's confessions. Restlessness certainly summed me up, and it was soon to turn into itchy feet.

~

Not long after my last fight in 1962, for no obvious reason, I started to think of travelling around Australia. I asked Eddie how he would feel about travelling with me—after all, he'd been my shadow in everything else.

Very significantly, my stepfather had been diagnosed with spinal cancer the year before and was now a semi-invalid, periodically undergoing treatment at the Peter MacCallum Cancer Centre in Melbourne. Since his diagnosis, the sordid, stormy scene at home had changed dramatically: the drunken parties had ceased, the domestic violence had ended, and the predators were no longer around. Now a pacifier rather than an aggressor, Ellis had stepped up substantially. He was working and living at a nearby farm, and he assured us that he would be filling in for us at home. Although my sister Val was working and living away from home, and my sister Denice had got married and also left home, both of them weren't all that far away and could come around regularly to help out. Eddie and I felt reassured that our family was safe and cared for.

We had no apprehension about travelling long distances. Living in rural Victoria as we were, it was second nature to us; the return distance from Wycheproof to Melbourne alone was more than three hundred miles.

Despite these assurances, we were quite emotional at the thought of going away. I had a lot to leave behind, as did Eddie. Although he was still living at home, and I wasn't, and was closer to our family than I was. Plus he'd started to play football and make more friends. Yet overriding everything was an exhilarating feeling of freedom. I imagined that getting out of prison after a long sentence would feel like this.

Victor was pretty stoic about his situation and encouraged Eddie to go. Mum and our siblings encouraged us too. 'Go and enjoy an adventure of a lifetime,' they said. That was it, the green light! We planned to leave in early April 1963, just before my twentieth birthday and Eddie's seventeenth. I traded my Austin A40 for a FC Holden ute and put a canopy on the back of it, and we were set to sail.

I would do all the driving, as Eddie was too young to get his licence. He was a very good and experienced driver, having done a lot of driving on farms and backroads around Wycheproof, but I was loath to let him drive on a major road during the day because we may have been pulled over by the police.

We would have a passenger: my purebred Scottish collie Prince. I'd purchased him off breeders who displayed dogs at shows, and that had sown a seed in me. I had decided to show him also, and groomed him and trained him to that end. He took a number of top placings in the brief time I showed him before he accompanied us on our travels.

~

Although Eddie and I were as convinced as we could be that things would be all right at home, it was a pretty heart-wrenching scene that confronted us the afternoon before we were due to drive off. It was a Sunday, and we planned to leave early the next morning. My stepfather was in a wheelchair looking old and frail. Six younger siblings were still living at home, ranging in age from fifteen to three, and while they would normally have been bounding about playing games with me and Eddie, they were pretty solemn during the afternoon and evening before they went to bed. The exception was three-year-old Ivan, who had no idea what was happening and played with us pretty normally, although Eddie and I found it hard to play. Val and Denice had come back to see us off and, while teary-eyed, assured us that they would keep an eye on the family and help out.

Eddie and I were up at five to leave at six, and as we were having breakfast all our siblings woke up and came out to see us off. Mum was already up. We said goodbye to my stepfather and insisted he stay in bed. Ellis came over from the farm he was working and living at to see us off also. He once again assured us that he would help out at home and was more emotional than I'd ever seen him. 'I need to stay and help,' he said, 'but I wish I was going with you. It'll be the trip of a lifetime.' It was a very emotional farewell.

We hit the road almost right on 6 a.m. Although we were still planning to explore as much of Australia as possible, we'd decided to drive around eight hundred miles straight up the Newell Highway to the town of St George in south-west Queensland. That was because Bernie Credlin—formerly of Wycheproof and a friend of Des Wood's—was the water board engineer in St George and had many contacts there. He owned considerable acreage of farmland around the town and had offered us part-time work there. He had also already arranged jobs for us at the Marouga Sawmill. It was too good an opportunity to pass up: we could make a lot of money in a few months and then travel extensively before we needed to work again.

There were some significant stops we felt we had to make. One was at the Murray River in Echuca just before the New South

Wales border, about two hours from Wycheproof. We wanted to view the mighty river, renowned for its codfish, and to see one of its famous paddle steamers. Eddie, a very keen and good fisherman, was in awe of the Murray cod, Australia's largest freshwater fish. The biggest ever landed, he'd heard, was six feet long and weighed 250 pounds. Unfortunately we didn't have time to give him the opportunity to break the record! We were fortunate, however, that a paddle steamer was moored at the jetty, so we were able to have a look. It was a fairly early one, *Pride of the Murray*, that had been plying its trade on the water since 1924.

Just up the road from Echuca was Tocumwal, with its historic railway bridge along the state border. Opened in 1895, the bridge had three spans, the middle one lifting up for high river traffic to pass under. As we approached Tocumwal I told Eddie about the Brisbane Line, which I'd recently read about. On 19 February 1942, Australia was under attack. Japan had just launched the first of sixty-four air strikes on Darwin, and our defence chiefs were alarmed. An invasion seemed imminent. Australia's defence appeared inadequate before the American forces arrived. After their arrival and joint strategic planning, a defence line was drawn between Brisbane and Melbourne, and Tocumwal was right in the middle of the line. Bomber bases were to be built along it, with the McIntyre Heavy Bomber Base to be a few miles out of Tocumwal. Property owners were given just twenty-four hours' notice before the compulsory acquisition of their land, some 5200 acres in total, while farm equipment was commandeered to frantically do the job. The base was completed in May 1942 and later became the RAAF Station Headquarters for training

Liberator Bomber aircrews. It was the largest aerodrome in the southern hemisphere.

The old airfield had closed as an RAAF base in 1960. Having talked it up, I could hardly not drive Eddie out to see it, or rather the remains of it. Although many aircraft hangars were still there, most of the houses had been shifted to the Canberra suburb of O'Connor because of a housing shortage there years before, and hundreds of aircraft had been broken up and scrapped. As a history buff, I thought it was still well worth visiting the site. Eddie appreciated it too. And just as importantly, Prince was glad of another walk and a toilet break. We had plenty of drink and eats on board, and we took time to have morning tea before heading off again. We didn't waste too much time, however—we still had some seven hundred miles to go.

~

Our next special interest stop was to be in Parkes, some five hours further north and about halfway from Wycheproof to St George.

Finley and Narrandera were new names to us as we drove through them. Jerilderie rang a bell, as I thought I could recall Ned Kelly having committed a crime there. It turned out I was right: he and three of his gang had carried out an audacious raid in the township, holding more than thirty residents hostage and entering the police barracks, where they locked up a senior constable and trooper in their own cell. The outlaws stole uniforms from the barracks, put them on, then went to the local blacksmith to get their horses shod and put it on the police account!

Arriving in Parkes about 4.30 p.m. was like passing the halfway mark of a gruelling marathon that had been uphill to this point and was now going to be downhill. Eddie cried out, 'Whoopee! Wow!' We had broken the back of the trip.

I wanted to check out the massive CSIRO Parkes Observatory. It had only been going for two years but was already making its mark on the world of astronomy. It had the first radio telescope built as a big moveable dish. 'Big' being the operative word—it was larger than two Boeing 747 aircraft! Amazingly it wasn't fixed to the tower, as its weight alone held it there. What fascinated me above everything else was the radio telescope's ability to eavesdrop in space.

Since childhood I'd been enthralled with the Buck Rogers and Flash Gordon space comic strips. When space travel became a reality, I was hooked. On the way to Parkes, Eddie had become my sounding-board for this fascination. 'Will we one day be able to travel in space like Buck Rogers?' 'Will we encounter life on other planets?' 'Will the Russians really rule the world from the moon?' My moon question came about because I'd read a prophetic claim by a preacher, not long before leaving on this trip, that Russia would be first to land on the moon and would take over the world from there. It was the height of the Cold War, and the race between Russia and America to be the first to place a man on the moon was intensifying. Cynical as I was then about outlandish religious claims, I not only thought but said, 'That preacher would want to be a true prophet and not a false one, because in biblical times a false prophet would have been stoned to death!'

Memory fails me, but either the Parkes Observatory had closed for the day or wasn't open to tourists at that stage. For whatever reason, we weren't able to go inside and look through the giant telescope. But to me, just seeing the huge structure was good enough.

~

In Parkes we bought a takeaway meal for ourselves and a treat for Prince, then decided to have our eats and let him have a run around at Bushmans Hill. Although we'd just passed the halfway mark, I planned to drive through the night as much as possible, my idea being that it would be good to arrive in St George early the next day. So we filled our jerry cans as well as the petrol tank before leaving town at 6 p.m.

There were a number of limitations on night driving, however. One was fatigue on my part, because I'd been doing all the driving. And as we drove further north, kangaroos became more of a potential hazard, especially at night and in the early morning. Only three years older than Eddie, my experience driving with the hazards of kangaroos was pretty limited.

The terrain had been relatively flat from Tocumwal to Narrandera, and since then it had been increasingly hilly and low-lying. Flood-measuring posts indicated that water could rise up to two metres over the road sometimes, but the surrounding paddocks were quite dry. That didn't auger well for us as far as kangaroos were concerned, because most of the greenery was on the side of roads untouched by stock in the paddocks, and hence roos would probably be there into the night, getting their fill.

During the drive from Parkes to Gilgandra we only saw a few kangaroos on the side of the road, most of them before the sun had gone down. It was quite nerve-racking, though, and we soon found out what the saying 'jumping at shadows' really means, especially after it got dark. Large boulders and bushes kept appearing along the roadside, which didn't help. On a couple of occasions kangaroos suddenly rushed across the road, but they were probably a hundred yards away so had plenty of time to avoid us.

Eddie was nodding off to sleep and jerked awake when I called out, 'What the hell?' and jerked the wheel to avoid a roo that either wasn't there or didn't jump out.

I realised I was driving dangerously. I'd hoped to make it to Coonabarabran before stopping for the night but decided to stop in Gilgandra at around 11 p.m. We parked at the footy oval and slept in the back of the ute. The Newell Highway was busy with transport trucks during the night, so we tried to get away from the highway to avoid their noise. We couldn't have been too far away from the highway, though, because although I had a deep sleep, I remember being suddenly woken by the sound of loud air-brakes being used, and the sound of Prince barking with fright as he heard them.

Early the next morning, we looked at our road map for the last leg of our journey. It struck us that most of the towns on the way had been named with Aboriginal words. This included Goondiwindi, the first Queensland town en route.

The drive there from Gilgandra took us about six hours, including a stop at Moree. We were just over a hundred miles to St George. We had lunch, did a final fuel-up, took Prince for a walk, and were ready for the last lap.

Eddie, meanwhile, had engaged a local in conversation and found out the English translation of 'Goondiwindi'. 'You won't believe it, Bill,' he said, unable to contain a huge grin and giggle.

'Tell me, then!'

'Well, it's two words really. Goondi means "droppings", and windi means "duck". In other words, "Goondiwindi" means "duck droppings"!'

'What? You mean "Goondiwindi" means "duck shit"?'

'Yes!'

We burst out laughing.

At the time I assumed the local Aboriginal people must have seen it as hilarious that Europeans had commandeered one of their words without knowing what it meant.

~

After the long trip from Wycheproof, the last leg from Goondiwindi to St George was more like the last ankle! There were just four little towns—almost ghost towns—on the way, with only a few hundred people in total in all of them. My mind was on what awaited us in St George and further afield. It was to be our gateway to the rest of Australia.

I couldn't wait to catch up with Des's mate Bernie again. He was a devout Catholic and a very caring person. Although he was busy in his engineering role, he'd asked us to let him know our estimated time of arrival so he could be waiting for us, and I'd rung him from Goondiwindi to tell him that we were only two or three hours away.

Approaching St George at first was almost like arriving back at Wycheproof. The temperature in April was in the high twenties, the terrain was flat and there were irrigation channels everywhere. The only difference was that the St George channels were bore drains, which flowed from artesian bores, and the water coming out of them was hot. Being the joker, I couldn't help saying to Eddie, 'I hope the hot bore water doesn't mean the people are red-hot boring!' Another notable feature was the cattle grids across the main road, indicating that there was probably cattle industry in the area. There were mixed emotions as we drove into St George at about 3.30 p.m. Being welcomed by Bernie Credlin, who was eager to hear of his relatives and friends back in Wycheproof, reminded us that we had left ours behind. A big lump formed in my throat and I'm sure in Eddie's too. On the other hand, Bernie represented provision of accommodation and employment and a known friend, and St George an exciting launching pad for further Australia-wide adventures.

Bernie seemed quite overjoyed to greet us. Having been in St George some ten years, he was really missing his family and friends back in Wycheproof. He was thirsty for up-to-date news from his hometown, especially about Des as well as the local footy. 'You must be hungry and thirsty,' Bernie said. 'How about leaving your gear in your ute for the moment, coming over to the staff tucker place and having some afternoon tea while I pick your brains about home?'

And that he did, for about half an hour, before he showed us to the very comfortable accommodation he'd organised for us at the Balonne Shire Council Barracks. Because St George was the largest town in the shire, the council provided accommodation for many shire workers from outlying areas.

The barracks were very basic but quite sufficient. There was a separate common-room with a kitchen and lounge room where visitors could be entertained, and a fairly large laundry with a number of washing machines. The cabins were small but adequate, consisting of a little combination kitchen/dining room, lounge room, and a sizable bedroom with two bunks.

Ideal for Eddie and me, well used to sharing rooms.

9

The winds of change

Bernie was a close friend of Senior Constable Ray Horne, a St George policeman who was keen to start a youth club there. He'd been weighing up between commencing a Police Youth and Citizens Youth Club or a National Fitness Club. Bernie had briefed him about my involvement in the Wycheproof youth club, and Eddie and I were both fit, athletic and enthusiastic young men. Constable Horne asked us to go to Toowoomba with him and weigh up the worth of the two types of club.

Although Eddie and I had been partial to the Wycheproof club, we were impressed with the National Fitness Club and opted towards it. There was a bigger range of general fitness activities, and I had a selfish motive too: weightlifting was an integral part of the club, and I now fancied myself as a competitive weight-lifter. Eddie and I soon found ourselves foundation members of the St George National Fitness Club. We periodically travelled with Horne to various National Fitness competitions around Queensland.

The club was housed in the St George Council Hall. It had a semicircular stage at the front with two doors underneath for a large storage area to stow away the equipment for every hall activity, including the folding chairs used when it was an occasional movie theatre. A weekly shuttle tennis competition was held there, and the two main fitness activities were gymnastics and weight training, including competitive weightlifting.

When Eddie first saw the stage, he got quite carried away about the weightlifting performances. 'Can't you see it, Bill? Lights, sound, action! We're pumping iron on the stage. You're Charles Atlas,' the famous Italian-born American bodybuilder, 'and I'm Mighty Mouse,' an animated superhero mouse. 'You're breaking records left, right and centre, lifting more than twice your body weight. I'm standing alongside you, literally over-shadowed by you. You decide to do a bit of a victory jump with the barbell and weights still held above your head. Then there's the crash of you falling through the stage floor, almost drowned out by the gasps of the audience—and their thunderous applause as Mighty Mouse grabs the huge barbell and weights before they smash into your skull.'

'Yeah, that'd be right,' I said, 'I can see the headline, "Mighty Mouse rescues Mighty Brawn"!'

I did go on to become a successful weightlifter in the club, hopefully using my brains as well as my brawn!

$\sim$

It was providential that Bernie had arranged jobs for me and Eddie at the Marouga Sawmill. Stan Fletcher, the joint owner and manager, hosted a Christian youth group for a Bible discussion at his home every Sunday afternoon. Through Stan they had heard of our pending arrival, and according to Bernie they were quite excited about it.

There was a slight case of mistaken identity. My precious FC Holden ute had a sticker on it with the letters CMS. Unbeknown to me it was a religious sticker, and the letters stood for Church Missionary Society. Members of the youth group saw the sticker and assumed my brother and I were religious. After my brief exploratory period of churchgoing in Wycheproof, I was still interested but certainly not religious, and Eddie wasn't either.

The reality was that although I'd been quite browned off and disillusioned by the hypocrisy of most churchgoers I knew, I could never get around the incredible faith of my mother, despite every attempt, particularly by my stepfather, to knock the faith out of her. Her faith had been crystallised for me by a major incident when I was a teenager. Mum was thrown through the windscreen of a car driven by my drunk stepfather, and she sustained serious facial and head injuries. Visiting her in hospital, I was very distraught at how terrible her injuries looked, and angry at my stepfather, but above all I blamed a God I didn't believe in for allowing it to happen. I said so to Mum in no uncertain terms: 'If there is a God, how could He have allowed something like this to happen?'

Mum responded through cut and swollen lips, and broken teeth. 'It doesn't matter what you think, Billy. There is a God, and I believe in Him.'

At times those words came back to haunt me and challenge me.

The group of religious young people in St George were quite different from those I had known in Wycheproof. Their Christianity wasn't confined to Sundays: they practised it every day of the week, with friendship and hospitality. Eddie and I had only been in town a couple of weeks when some members of the youth group, passing by on the footpath, told us they were off to play badminton and invited us to join them. The game was to be played in the local Church of England hall where some of the group attended church. Being general sports lovers, my brother and I gladly accepted the invitation.

A girl by the name of Beverley Beaton was there, a dark-haired, fair-skinned shy young lady with a beautiful smile. I could hardly take my eyes off her. I had heard and read of love at first sight, and wondered if it could really happen, but it did for me.

Not long after the badminton meet-up, the youth group invited me and Eddie to join them for a picnic and a swim at the Balonne River. The river and its surrounds were idyllic. The stream was very wide and surprisingly clear, the water was temperate and the bottom sloped gently into deeper areas. It was ideal for swimming. The town side was lined with lots of trees and spacious picnicking areas, which were very popular. It was a BYO lunch from memory, and Bev brought fish and chips to share with Eddie and me. That was a particularly memorable day for me, because Bev stood out like a rose in the desert. Feeling emboldened, I asked her if I could take her to the movies. She was just sixteen, but she accepted—on the condition that I meet her parents, and that they agreed.

They did, but only after her mother gave me a stern talking-to about how Bev was only sixteen, not old enough to be too serious.

I was to bring her home straight after the movie, around 11 p.m. 'Make sure you do,' Mrs Beaton said. 'This lantern will be burning and not put out until Beverley is home and safely in bed. Someone will come looking for you if you're not here on time.' This gave me nightmares, as I kept visualising a lantern-bearing grim reaper coming after me in the darkness because I hadn't got Bev home on time! In reality I accepted the conditions of dating Bev and mostly kept to the deadline.

Bev's family were marvellous to me and Eddie. When Mrs Beaton realised that this bachelor pair could hardly cook to save ourselves, she took us under her wing and spoilt us. In turn I helped outside the house where I could, but my enthusiasm to mow the lawns for her almost backfired badly. I mistook one of her precious plants for a weed and mowed it to the ground. She did forgive me but looked at me at first as if I was some ignorant Victorian who didn't know a plant from a weed!

Mr Beaton owned a tyre business, along with his son Ted, servicing everything from pushbikes and motorbikes to tractors and trucks. Eddie and I assisted Bev's dad with renovations to the family home, which had once been a school. It was weatherboard surrounded by wide verandas, and we helped build a room by enclosing part of a veranda.

There were six children in the Beaton family: Bev, three sisters and two brothers. Ted, Eric and Glenis were older than Bev, and Sherril and Julianne were younger. Eddie and I got to know them all quite well, because their mum invited us to regular meals and made us part of her extended family.

~

Stan Fletcher proved to be a vital spiritual link for me. While working alongside me at the sawmill, he soon became aware that I was seeking deeper meaning in life. He was very discerning in his approach—he didn't hit me over the head with Bible quotes but rather sowed seeds that helped me reflect on my need for something more fulfilling. Over smokos and lunchbreaks, he drew me out by asking about my background and interests, especially in sport, and asking what had satisfied me and what hadn't. The reality was that all my sporting pursuits had satisfied me, but only for a time.

Stan's children were part of the group that attended the weekly Bible discussions at his home. He invited me and Eddie along, telling me that Bev went there also. I needed no other inducement! But Eddie didn't go—he hung out with Bev's sister Sherril instead. She was also a stunning beauty: dark haired, dimple cheeked, and a bit taller than Bev. Eddie was short and slight at that stage, but he had a magnificent head of curly blond hair and was very handsome. He tended to be a real chick magnet.

Jack Evans and his wife Ollie led the Bible discussions. It's an interesting coincidence that now I'd had a Godfrey and an Evans cross my path. Godfrey Evans! Mr Godfrey my teacher and encourager, and Jack Evans my spiritual mentor. The Evans were home missionaries of the Presbyterian church that the Fletchers attended. Jack appealed to me because he'd been a fighter pilot in World War II. After flying dangerous missions over Germany, he'd found religion late in life.

The youth group invited me to join them at a church camp at Table Top Mountain, Toowoomba, a couple of hundred miles from

St George, and I was happy to go. It was great to be with Bev and her friends, and to be accepted by them, warts and all.

At the camp there were some Church of England ministers from Sydney who were quite different from the one in St George. I learnt that they were known as 'low Anglican' rather than 'high Anglican'. The latter tended to be very formal, burning incense and performing rituals, while the former were more down-to-earth and practical.

I taught one of these ministers how to play hoppo-bumpo, a game I used to play at school in the shelter sheds. One student would stand in the middle of the shed, while all the others stood at one end. The one in the centre nominated a student to try and hop past him to the other end. Both had to keep their arms tightly folded and hop on one leg without putting the other down. The goal was to bump the nominated student off his feet before he got past you; if you didn't, everyone could hop through to try and reach the other end. If you bumped anyone off their feet, they joined you in the centre and helped you.

During a walk from our camp site to the summit of Table Top Mountain, I explained the game to a visiting minister who was dressed casually but had his white clerical collar on. 'Let's have a go here,' he said abruptly.

I was quite surprised—to this point I'd only known ministers who were fairly aloof and didn't want to interact with young people in ways like this. 'Okay,' I said, 'try and hop past me.'

All of a sudden the clerical collar became like a red rag to a bull. The minister hopped alongside of me fairly fast, and by the pleased look on his face I could tell he thought he'd made it. This game was second nature to me, however, and I was used to catching my prey in a boxing ring. As he glanced over at me, I quickened my hops and hit him with a very solid hip and shoulder. He was sent sprawling into a prickly lantana bush.

The venom of my hit shocked me, and I think him also, as well as Bev and her friends, but he was as good-natured and forgiving about the incident as I was apologetic. He won my admiration for having a go. This helped to change my opinion about men of the cloth. It also occurred to me that I'd taken out my frustrations on a representative of a God I wasn't sure existed.

Little did I know that on the heels of this camp the wheels were in motion for a dramatic change in my destiny.

~

Bev and I were going together steadily and were pretty insepar-able. However, we were to be in different places from early January 1964 until the third week of that month. Bev went to a Chris-tian convention in Port Macquarie, while Eddie and I stayed in St George, except when we ventured out one weekend to a weightlifting competition in Toowoomba.

The fourteenth of January 1964 stands out in my memory for a couple of notable reasons. Firstly, it was Bev's seventeenth birthday, and secondly, one of the most significant events in St George's history occurred on that day. I woke up early thinking of Bev and the amazing impact she'd had on my life in the brief year I had known her. Then I tried to ring her and wish her Happy Birthday but no one was answering the phone at her camp site. The more I thought about her devout spirituality, the more dissatisfied I felt. Then the indelible words of Augustine came back to me: 'Our hearts are restless until we find our rest in God.'

As I often did when feeling down, I went for a run, hoping to leave my concerns behind. Eddie was still asleep. Throughout the night it had been fairly windy, and while I was out the wind intensified noticeably.

It was just as well all the other guys in the barracks had gone home for Christmas, because when I got back Eddie had the new Beatles single 'I Want to Hold Your Hand' blasting away on the radio. This just made me miss Bev more.

My brother and I had breakfast together and planned to go fishing in the Balonne. The yellow-belly were biting, evidently. Bev's brother Eric was the source of this information, a master fisherman who was ever out in his tinnie.

But our expedition never eventuated. Cyclone Audrey struck with great ferocity at 8 a.m. Winds roared and whistled in, and torrential rain followed.

The cyclone made itself viciously known in St George by blasting off or badly damaging the roofs of fifty-two houses and severely damaging twenty-two business premises. No lives were lost, fortunately. The local police had driven around just before the wind intensified, telling people to batten down and shelter in secure areas, and many had gone into the large coldroom at the butcher's.

Eddie and I, foolishly, were oblivious to the danger. With the wind and rain still very intense, we drove around observing and photographing the damage. Bev's family home was unscathed, but her brother Eric's house had the weatherboards stripped off the sides like dry bark from trees, although amazingly the roof stayed on. A row of sizeable trees in front of the primary school were completely flattened.

Bev arrived back from Port Macquarie very relieved that none of her family members had been injured, that Eddie and I were all right too, and that her home wasn't damaged. She then told me why no one answered the phone on her birthday. They hadn't heard of the cyclone affecting St George but were warned that it was coming down the coast to Port Macquarie. Bev and the rest of the campers were assembled in an emergency shelter and couldn't take phone calls. Fortunately, the cyclone didn't reach them. She had enjoyed the conference very much and shared some of the highlights with us the following Sunday afternoon.

The winds of change were also blowing strongly in my personal life. I was obsessed with training for the coming weightlifting titles, and I kept skipping church and the Bible discussion group, so Bev and I were seeing each other less frequently. For some reason I became increasingly grumpy and foul-mouthed, which didn't make me pleasant company.

One day the motor in my ute seized up, and I started frantically putting a new one in. I was doing this work around the side of Bev's home, and Mrs Beaton warned everyone in the household not to go out there: 'Bad language and tools and all sorts of things are being thrown around.'

Bev and Eddie heeded her advice, and they went for a long drive with Sherril and a couple of Bev's friends. That was the straw that broke the camel's back—after that, Bev and I stopped going out together.

~

Not being with Bev regularly was hell for me, especially because Eddie was still going out with Sherril. My situation wasn't helped by Stan, who kept me updated on the discussion group and, of course, Bev. Easter was fast approaching, and Stan told me there was going to be a special Easter camp on a farm just outside St George. Would I like to go? There was going to be a great speaker from the China Inland Mission, and Bev would be there!

So I found myself at another church camp. I can't remember a word the speaker said, but he hung up a poster in the meeting room that really resonated with me and continues to speak to me. It was a picture of an old Chinese man struggling up a steep mountainside with a large pack on his back. I felt it represented me: I was carrying all the baggage of my past, which was getting heavier by the minute, while I became more and more frustrated.

Although Bev and I saw a lot of each other over the camp weekend, we didn't get back together. We were so near and yet so far apart.

The following Saturday evening, Jim Mitchell—the president of the National Fitness Club—invited me and Eddie out to his farmhouse for dinner. When we walked in, all of a sudden Bev and her friends came out of hiding, shouting in chorus, 'Happy birthday!' Bev had planned my surprise twenty-first birthday party before we broke up and felt obligated to follow it through.

I couldn't remember ever having a birthday party before. It was quite overwhelming. Not only were Bev and I back together again, at least for the evening, but there was also an amazing feeling of love, acceptance and family. I had already started to get a strong sense of family in contrast to my own—through meeting families like the Beatons, the Fletchers and the Evanses.

Much fun and laughter and pure enjoyment, rather than alcohol and arguments and violence and sordidness, filled our time that evening. A great variety of games had been organised, including limbo, a traditional West Indian game. To participate you had to manoeuvre under a broomstick while bending backwards without ducking, and for every successful underpass the broom was lowered further. The person to get under at the lowest point was the winner.

Throughout the course of the evening, I had a strange experience. Some words kept coming into my head: *Don't get sidetracked or you'll go after vain things that won't really satisfy you or fulfil you.* I'd been told that hearing voices was a sign of insanity, so I hoped I wasn't losing my mind!

Jim's wife had made a scrumptious creamed sponge cake, and placed on top was a beautiful weightlifting image that she'd sculpted out of icing. Before the cutting of the cake, speeches were made, and Jim's was the highlight. He'd made a miniature set of metal barbells in the form of a twenty-first birthday key. Holding it up, he said he hoped it would represent success and happiness in every area of my life, beginning with the weightlifting title I'd be contesting later that month. Jim said he was thrilled to see a group of fine young people embracing me as their friend and that he hoped they would be a strong foundation for my future: 'Because we can't make it on our own, and we need good people around us.'

The party ended just after 11 p.m. Eddie and I dropped Bev home and went back to our barracks to get ready for bed. Despite being surrounded by religious people, and the fact Sherril hadn't attended the party, Eddie said he'd had a ball. Love and acceptance on this scale would have been new to him also.

Do you think I could go to sleep? No way. Bright images of the party kept flashing before my mind's eye like a beacon—images of Bev especially, accompanied by a longing for us to be back together. Contrasting images of the good and the bad from my past kept coming to me too, and then the negative started to prevail over the positive. Resentment and anger welled up in me for all the love I had been deprived of and all the pain that had been inflicted on me. Vengeful thoughts, such as I had not experienced in a long time, came to mind.

In the midst of these thoughts, I had a vision of Jesus on the cross. He was speaking to me, saying, 'Forgive them, for they didn't know what they were doing.'

'What?' I blurted out. 'Like hell they didn't know what they were doing!'

I was arguing with the voice of someone I wasn't sure even existed, and yet I was being gripped by a figure and authority I couldn't deny.

'Bill, forgiveness is not about them, it's about you. Has *not* forgiving helped you?'

I remembered the poster of the elderly Chinese man. The weight of all my hatred and bitterness and non-forgiveness was unbearable. All of a sudden no one and nothing else mattered, just me and my enormous burden. I started to cry.

Since childhood I had steeled and insulated myself against emotional pain. I had cried on a few notable occasions, but I'd always clung to the notion that 'big men don't cry'. Now all the years of bottled-up emotion overflowed and gushed out of me.

I made a simple but heartfelt request. 'Jesus, I don't know if you're real, but if you are, prove yourself. I hate what I've become. Change me—make me a better person.'

Suddenly a deep peace came over me, and I fell asleep.

~

At work in the sawmill the following day, I wasn't thinking about what had occurred the night before. That was until near the end of the day, when the bloke pulling the timber away from me as I gauged logs asked, 'What's the matter with you? Are you sick or something?'

'What do you mean? Why?'

'You haven't sworn or flown off the handle or thrown anything around all day!'

It was then that I realised something extraordinary had happened. The bad-tempered, foul-mouthed, angry young man really had changed. I had never heard the phrase of Jesus, 'You must be born again,' but clearly I had been! My heart of hate and bitterness and non-forgiveness had been replaced with a heart of love and peace and forgiveness.

When I finished the day's work I told Stan what had happened and explained that I was now experiencing a peace I had never known before. 'The Lord has come into your life,' he told me. 'The Bible says, "If anyone is in Christ, they are a new person, old things have passed away and all things have become new." You've become a Christian. Welcome to the family! The young people, and especially Bev, are going to be thrilled.' He advised me to pray and read the Bible regularly. He even gave me a Bible.

10

The fruit of change

Following my conversion, Bev and I got back together. We now had spirituality in common, and I was over the moon. Attending church and going to the Bible discussion group took on new meaning for me. Previously I'd gone mainly because I wanted to spend more time with Bev. Now I also wanted to learn more about Jesus, who had indeed proved himself to me. When I told the group what had happened in my life, they were thrilled. They told me that I was now a member of the family of God, and that they were my brothers and sisters and would be there for me. I couldn't have been happier.

To my amazement, Jack Evans told me that the words that had come to me during my birthday party were very similar to some from the Bible. Jack and Ollie were a great help to me as spiritual mentors, giving me tips for spiritual growth like having a 'quiet time' first thing in the morning to pray and read the Bible.

They also taught me to memorise helpful Bible verses in alphabetical order.

By mid-1964 I was champing at the bit to do more with my new-found Christian experience. Bev was conducting a Sunday school for children at an Aboriginal reserve on the outskirts of St George, so I started to go there with her. Bev's parents had sold their tyre service and built the first supermarket in south-west Queensland. It was staffed mostly by their children, including Bev. The Beatons saved all the dented tins—containing a great variety of food—for the local Aboriginal people, plus a lot of leftover fruit and vegetables. The practical help and spiritual hope that Bev delivered each week struck a real chord with them. This work appealed to me, because although as a new Christian I didn't know much about the Bible, I could occasionally tell the story of my own difficult background and changed life, and it seemed to register with them. The story of my time as a former boxer and current weight-lifter really grabbed their attention.

Then Jack asked me, 'What do you want to do with your life now, Bill?'

'Go back to the people of my background and share with them how my life has changed' was my answer.

The Evanses had done their initial training at the Melbourne Bible Institute or MBI before becoming Presbyterian home missionaries, and they suggested I might consider doing similar training. This made sense to me, because an integral part of the training involved lots of different Christian work experiences, which hopefully would help me to find my niche. I was accepted into a two-year Diploma of Christian Education at MBI, to commence in February 1965.

Part of the course consisted of studying the New Testament Greek language, and that put a cat among the pigeons in my mind. Only having had up to a Grade Six education, I was barely proficient in English, let alone able to study Greek. Enter Bev. 'You can do it,' she encouraged me. 'I can help you to brush up on English so that by the end of the year you'll know enough to study Greek.' Bev was a great teacher, and English was her forte, so she helped me to progress in leaps and bounds. She knew grammar and spelling like the back of her hand—I'd never known anyone who could spell like she could. And the big bonus was that I could spend a lot of additional time alongside her!

Being back with Bev and on her spiritual wavelength was another turning point in my life. It had been love at first sight for me with Bev, and I'd been aware from the moment I met her that there was a deeper quality about her. Her beauty wasn't just skin-deep. The more I got to know her the more that was confirmed.

Bev had broken off our relationship previously because of her belief that we were 'unequally yoked', a concept from the Bible: we were like two oxen harnessed together but pulling in opposite directions. At the time she was correct, but now things were vastly different. I was absolutely convinced that God had brought us together and that Bev was my soulmate.

~

Soon after my twenty-first birthday, Eddie returned to Wycheproof. His father was terminally ill, and Eddie wanted to make the most of their remaining time together. At the end of September, Victor deteriorated badly. He was rushed back to hospital in Melbourne and died on 5 October 1964. On the night her father died, Jeannie was having her first ever school social, and Eddie had the unenviable task of going there and informing her of her dad's death. She was fourteen.

I decided to drive down to Wycheproof for my stepfather's funeral and then remain there until the start of my diploma. Prince had stayed with me in St George and had loved having me to himself in the council barracks. He'd also enjoyed being feted by Bev's family, especially her mum. Now he was very excited as we headed south to Victoria—it was as if he sensed that our circumstances were about to change dramatically.

Other than making a few necessary stops, I drove straight from St George to Wycheproof. It rained heavily through Queensland and well into New South Wales. While I was paying for fuel in Dubbo, a local priest was doing the same. I said, 'Hi there,' before I walked back to my ute.

The rain was pouring down. I didn't realise he'd followed me until I opened the ute door and Prince growled like a grizzly bear, attempting to launch past me.

A loud '*Aaaaahhh!*' sounded behind me. I closed the ute door and turned around, and there was the priest. 'Oh, sorry,' he said. 'Didn't realise you had such a devoted bodyguard!'

I told Prince to be quiet, and the priest asked where I was going and why I was driving through the night. When I told him I was rushing down for my stepfather's funeral, he said quite frankly, 'Son, if you don't have a break, they might be holding *your* funeral.' It was enough to cause me to have a break.

I slept the sleep of the dead for two hours, until the squawking of air brakes on a truck woke me up. I couldn't go back to sleep, but my mind was fresh and alert, going ten to the dozen as I contemplated my stepfather's life. There was no escaping the reality of all his abuse of me and others, but I was amazed at my forgiving and understanding attitude. I thought of how he'd run away from home at a very young age and probably endured great hardship on the voyage out to Australia, possibly suffering physical violence and sexual abuse himself. He'd survived the horror of hell on earth at Anzac Cove; the loss of his farm during the Great Depression; the suicide of his first wife, and the placement of all his children in homes. I couldn't forget the 'whats' of his terrible wrongdoing, but I wondered about the 'whys' of the making of the man and the moulding of his behaviour.

Arriving home after nearly two years away, I stayed with Mum in her new home on the outskirts of town. It wasn't far from the quarry where Powder-Monkey Jimmy's caravan had been, now long since gone, the place from where Eddie and I had launched off for many mischievous exploits. Mum had moved house while my stepfather was having long stays in the Peter MacCallum Cancer Centre. She was quite isolated out at the old property on the Avoca River, some ten miles from Wycheproof. Mum couldn't drive and Eddie and Ellis were both working away and weren't available to drive her, so it was much more convenient to live in town. In addition, Mrs Wood's commitment to Charlie before he died, to look after me, extended to my family also, and she undertook to give mum respite by having the girls stay over with her periodically. She was thrilled to have me home for the three months before I was to start studying at MBI, as were my siblings. There were still six kids at home, now ranging in age from sixteen to four.

Ellis had really tried to make amends to Mum and support her in our absence. He'd become the handyman around the home. In the process of painting the house, he'd fallen off an improvised trestle and broken an ankle. He was off crutches but still limping a little bit when I arrived home.

It had been a tough homecoming for Eddie. He was only eighteen but had needed to become the man of the house while his father was in hospital and to help care for him when he was at home recuperating between treatments. Eddie was very work oriented and had already got himself a good job with a concreter in Wycheproof.

The funeral was a pretty big one for a small town, and the Anglican church was crowded. Our immediate and extended family alone just about filled it. My stepfather was a noted ex-serviceman from both the first and second world wars, and most of the RSL members from Wycheproof were present. One of them conducted the final part of the graveside service with the words 'lest we forget', then a bugler played 'The Last Post'.

Des sat alongside me at the funeral service, and I'll never forget his comment afterwards about my singing of 'The Lord's My Shepherd'. 'Bill, you sang that hymn with such sincerity and belief. I can't believe how much you have changed.'

~

Mum's household was a strange one after my stepfather's funeral. It was a home fairly devoid of emotion. The youngest two children, Lila and Ivan, were too little to realise what had happened, and in any case Ellis did a great job distracting them by taking them on outings.

While Ellis got back to painting the house, Mum threw herself into establishing both a vegetable garden and a flower garden. She loved gladioli and set about planting those bulbs first. She was singing more now, but her songs had changed from being mostly those about prayer and a need for help and strength to those of thanksgiving and praise. 'Count Your Blessings' was her signature song, and it became indelibly impressed upon me also.

Despite Mum's brave exterior, Jeannie told me that she would sometimes come across her sitting with her head in her hands quietly sobbing. But Mum would never talk about her grief. She did what she had done throughout all her years of being abused: steeled herself and distracted herself to survive.

She was thrilled to have me home with her for a few months, and I thoroughly enjoyed joining her in song and prayer. She was as proud as punch that she now had a son on her spiritual wavelength, and she just about burst with pride when she introduced me to someone and told them her Billy was going to be a minister.

Jeannie, Gladys and Norma were enjoying their new-found freedom without their father around. He had been a fierce disciplinarian, so they were kicking up their heels a bit. Gordon had just finished a good season playing football with the Wycheproof under eighteens and was building a reasonable social network. Eddie was throwing himself into learning the ropes of the very strenuous job of concreting.

~

The person who was probably most moved by the change in my life was Ellis. He had been a violent drunk and my stepfather's worst henchman, yet I had forgiven him and only wanted to be friends with him.

Along with the incredible change in my life, the God-given capacity to forgive Ellis was a miracle. I could easily have killed him and the stepbrother who had sexually abused me—I'd thought of doing so a number of times. Things were very different now. After arriving back from Queensland, I really was a new person with new understandings and new attitudes. The words 'Forgive them, for they didn't know what they were doing' were ever with me. I still struggled with the thought, but I knew Jesus was right. His words to me on the night of my conversion—'Bill, forgiveness is not about them, it's about you'—made sense. Non-forgiveness was self-destructive for me: the hatred, anger and depression it caused were unbearable, and I had been quite suicidal at times. It probably would have cost me my life if things hadn't changed, or at least cost me a life wasted in prison.

But things had changed, dramatically. There was now great peace in my life, reflected in my singing. Like Mum, I found myself doing this often and spontaneously, a great release for my tension and a terrific uplifter for my heart and mind.

My singing was put to the test early one morning while I was staying in Mum's bungalow. Prince had been sleeping at the foot of my bed. All of a sudden I was woken by his loud barking, interspersed with savage growling usually reserved for when perceived danger was close at hand. I sprang out of bed and put on some shoes, then let Prince out and followed him.

Silhouetted against Mum's eastern fence, someone was retreating with what appeared to be a shotgun in hand. Prince was going berserk and raced towards the figure, who was escaping over the fence. I made a decision to quickly shut Prince in my room and follow the intruder.

I could see the shadowy figure walking down the road up ahead of me, and I wondered why this person didn't try harder to get away. It was early on a Sunday, about 1 or 2 a.m., and I was conscious of not wanting to wake up the whole neighbourhood, so I commenced walking swiftly after the intruder without saying a word.

We were soon well out of town, in farmland that I knew like the back of my hand. There were no farmhouses for a couple of kilometres. Then I did a strange thing—I started to sing. I can only imagine how weird he must have thought this was, but he kept walking. And I kept gaining on him, singing everything I could think of, especially Mum's favourite hymn 'What a Friend We Have in Jesus' and Mrs Beaton's favourite 'When We Walk with the Lord'.

I had nearly caught up to the person, clearly a male. 'Hey, mate,' I called out, 'let's talk. You were in our backyard, but probably by mistake.' Not that I really believed it.

He almost stopped and partly turned around, then kept walking. It looked like he had a shotgun pushed up the front of his jacket, the butt partly protruding. I was at his mercy now, not close enough to grab him but too close if he decided to turn around and shoot.

My internal prayer defence was working overtime—so was my tongue! 'Buddy, you must be feeling as cold as I am. I've just come back to Wyche for my stepdad's funeral, and I haven't been home for a fair while, so I wouldn't know what's going on. But I think I know what you might be going through. I've been through a fair bit myself.' I was trying to talk him down in any way I could, wearing my whole heart on my sleeve. 'Is that a gun under your jacket? What's with that?'

He stopped and turned around. 'Sorry, mate. I'll leave the fire stick up my jacket if you don't mind. It's not loaded, and I don't have any cartridges anyway.' Light misty rain was falling, and he probably wanted to keep the gun dry anyway.

The guy was quite young, more than likely in his late teens. His story was that there had been a very boisterous party at his parents' house. The more alcohol was consumed the more arguments started and tempers flared. A savage fight had broken out, and his dad had produced a gun. He'd snatched the gun off his dad and run before a tragedy could occur. All of this resonated with me—it was my childhood being relived.

The problem was that his story didn't really explain why he'd been in our backyard. His explanation—that the moon had gone behind a cloud while he was near our house, and before he knew it he had meandered off the road and through our open side gate—didn't ring true. He would have known immediately that he'd stepped off the bitumen road and onto the gravel of our driveway. He would have stopped until the moon came out again, in case he walked into a barbed-wire fence along the side of the road.

Nevertheless, with my Christian charity in its infancy, I gave him the benefit of the doubt and walked back into town with him. I asked him about his background and shared some of mine. I was an eager evangelist—perhaps overzealous—as I told the story of my changed life and that of Ellis's. We stopped outside Mum's house, and I prayed for him. We shook hands and parted, never to meet again.

~

While staying with Mum, I was invited to speak at Granite Flat Community Church, a tiny non-denominational church in a paddock several miles from Wycheproof. A couple of members of the church had studied at MBI and, having heard of my conversion and enrolment at the institute, were keen to hear my story.

The church was packed, mostly with farmers but also with some townspeople who had come out to listen to 'one of the Sutcliffes' tell his story. They were all eager to hear one of the black sleep of the area speak of a remarkably changed life, and they were soon to marvel at not just the power but also the miracle of forgiveness. That was my emphasis, and my stepbrother seemed to be riveted to every word.

Ellis was particularly moved by the marvellous singing of the great old hymn 'Bringing in the Sheaves'. I'd heard it sung in St George but never with so many voices, such gusto and such local relevance. In paddocks outside the church were hundreds of acres of glistening heads of wheat, which in older days would have been tied in sheaves and stood up like teepees in stooks or bundles throughout the paddocks.

Sowing in the morning,
Sowing seeds of kindness,
Sowing in the noontide,
   and the dewy eve.
Waiting for the harvest,
   and the time of reaping,
We shall come rejoicing,
Bringing in the sheaves.

After some great hospitality and a scrumptious lunch of country cooking, Ellis and I headed home. We were very pensive on the way back; hardly a word was spoken other than about how friendly and down-to-earth the church service had been in contrast to the high Anglican one in Wycheproof. To my pleasant surprise, Ellis said he'd like to go along to a special evangelistic weekend at the Granite Flat Church in a fortnight's time. The guest evangelist was going to be a man named Noel Smith.

Two weeks later, Ellis and I headed back to the church. The old church was packed to overflowing with both regulars and guests like me and Ellis. I was familiar with Christian camps but not with evangelistic rallies like this one. I needn't have worried, though: there was an uplifting and inspirational atmosphere with quality music and songs. Noel was billed as the 'Singing Evangelist', and sing he could. My stepbrother was particularly impressed because like Ellis's brother Tom, Noel was a rich baritone.

I don't remember what Noel spoke on, but I can still visualise Ellis being spellbound at his address and saying to me afterwards that he felt the evangelist was speaking only to him. At the end of the service Ellis disappeared, and Norm Bish, one of the organisers, told me that Noel was counselling him.

When Ellis came out from that session, his face was radiant. There's a quaint phrase in an old version of the Bible about how Moses looked when he came down from Mount Sinai after meeting God: 'Moses wist not that his face shone', or he didn't know that his face was shining. Ellis didn't know that his face was shining either.

My stepbrother was a completely changed man from that day on, totally giving up smoking and drinking and violence, and replacing them with love and joy and peace.

~

God was indeed proving Himself to me. I had read some words of the Apostle Paul in the Bible, 'My God shall supply all your need', and I believed that He was doing precisely that.

To help pay my MBI tuition fees I sold my beloved FC Holden, the faithful ute that had carried me and Eddie on our great adventure. I also sold my pine plantation shares to Des. The MBI policy was that even if you had enough money to pay your annual fees, you were still required to have a part-time job, and Des offered me one back on the farm until I commenced at MBI in February the following year, 1965. He also offered me a job during term breaks and Christmas holidays, and whenever I needed work for the two years that I would be in MBI. This was very generous of him and took a lot of pressure off me. And it was very nostalgic to work for Des again and to catch up with Mrs Wood, who had shifted off the farm into a house in town. (I had kept in touch with Des while I was away. Writing letters to find out how things were going at his end and letting him know how I was getting on where I was. Similarly I corresponded with his mother.)

Des had indeed kept his promise to his dad to look after me. He'd become an extension of Charlie, mentoring me and encouraging me to do the very best I could at anything I attempted—and to use my head as well as my hands. Mrs Wood had been a great help to Mum while my stepfather was sick, giving her and my sisters respite by having one of them stay overnight with her periodically. On the one hand I was sad moving on and away from them, but on the other I felt I was taking their motivation and inspiration with me to MBI, and that they could be proud that I was substantially a product of that.

I had resumed work on Des's farm as if I had never left. This time, however, I didn't live at the farm; I stayed at Mum's to maximise my time with her and my siblings. It was different but enjoyable to go home each night and catch up with them in the months before I commenced college. Who would know where I would work after graduation?

~

Attending MBI was a huge cultural change for me. From a background of bitter atheism I had made a massive shift into devout Christian belief, while most of the other students were from a Christian background. However, I was made to feel very much at home. It was also a big cultural shock for me to be living in Melbourne. As a small-town country boy from an early age, just catching trams and travelling shoulder to shoulder with commuters was quite an ordeal. But living at the MBI campus in the leafy, relatively quiet suburb of Armadale softened the blow considerably and certainly provided just the peaceful atmosphere I needed for study.

This was my first experience of needing to concentrate on lectures, take notes and then have exams. Fortunately, I was very good at retention. After one of my early exams, I was very surprised to get a relatively high mark of seventy-nine. My lecturer met me in a corridor and congratulated me. I didn't have the heart to tell him that I hadn't looked at my notes until I'd crammed the night before! I did knuckle down and become reasonably disciplined after that, though.

My first year at Bible college was incredible but surreal. I felt as if I was dreaming of being in a giant religious bubble that had floated me into an entirely new world—a strange world, a foreign world. It was also an exciting and wonderful world, and one that I felt I was meant to be in, because this was my destiny.

It was reinforced in me during the year, as my belief deepened and my confidence grew, that I had an important contribution to make in the world; that, as Powder-Monkey Jimmy had instilled in me, the seeming deficits of my life were my greatest assets. We had regular guest speakers at college who whet my appetite for Christian work that was close to my heart. I had a strong leaning towards those who were down and out, considered by society to be 'no-hopers', including the marginalised, the disenfranchised, those in the lowest socioeconomic groups, alcoholics, drug addicts, homeless people . . . in other words, people from my own background! Before the year was out I had offers to manage an alcoholic rehabilitation centre in Western Australia and to teach sawmilling to Papua New Guineans, which was amazing. News travels fast, and Bible colleges, like other institutions, are approached by potential employers to find out what expertise their students have. It would have been known that I had a family background of alcoholism and experience in sawmilling. While I was not comfortable with either of the offers, both were very accommodating and prepared to wait until I finished my studies. I was learning fast the spiritual application of 'When in doubt don't'; 'Let the peace of God rule in your heart'.

As the year advanced, so did my ability to achieve, academically and practically. However, I was sometimes overcome with thoughts that I'd deserted my mother, my siblings and Prince, and I would be beside myself with guilt. But Mum always encouraged me to prioritise what God wanted me to do above everything else. She said it was like a horse and cart—if I put God first, everything else would follow behind. Some timely words of the Apostle Paul jumped out at me from the Bible: 'Everything works together for good to those who love God and are called according to His purpose.' My belief in this idea gave me a deep peace about Mum, my siblings and Prince being cared for.

In September, Mum sold up in Wycheproof. She and most of the family, including Prince, shifted to Eildon, while Eddie stayed behind to work at his concreting job. Eildon is east of Alexandra, on the southern shores of Lake Eildon at the Goulburn River. This scenic spot is surrounded by a national park and mountains covered in thick forests. Mum's sister and brother-in-law, who lived in Alexandra, had been encouraging her to shift closer to them following the death of my stepfather. Mum, my family and Prince settled in very happily, and I was able to visit them a couple of times before the end of the year. Prince was a very good watch dog for Mum.

I think being at peace about my family and Prince enabled me to settle comfortably into my comprehensive college work experience for the rest of my time at MBI. That was to give Christian education in a primary school, to conduct an open-air Sunday School, and to work with the Salvation Army Chaplain in Pentridge Prison. I loved relating to young people in school and out in the open air. I mainly taught grades five and six, and students really warmed to my sporting background and the turnaround of my life. Teachers would say, 'That's a tough class, Bill, but they're eating out of your hand!'

Visiting prisons was my niche. Imagine having work experience in prison! I worked with Brigadier Peterson in Pentridge Prison. The fifties and sixties were dramatic years in Pentridge. William O'Meally, who I met with Brigadier Peterson, was still serving time there. He was charged with murdering a policeman in 1952 and was sentenced to hang. That was later commuted to life imprisonment, but he was then granted parole after 27 years, becoming Australia's longest serving prisoner. I also met Ronald Ryan, who escaped from Pentridge the first year I was visiting, in 1965. A prison officer was killed during the escape and Ryan was convicted of his murder and hanged. It was the impetus for the abolition of capital punishment. He was the last person to be hanged in Victoria.

11

Two are better than one

Bev was incredibly supportive throughout my first year at college. She told me that I was doing remarkably well and that she was very proud of me, and especially how much she loved me and identified with me.

Bev and I had a very matter-of-fact relationship. Because of how we had bonded, it was almost taken for granted that we would marry each other and do Christian work together. We spoke like that and corresponded like that. I intended to travel to Queensland at the end of the year and formally propose to her.

For her sake, though, I needed to be sure she knew what she was letting herself in for. If she agreed to marry me, she would do so with her eyes open. So I wrote and told her so, outlining the scenarios that could occur should she marry me and work with me. We could finish up in any of the slum areas of the world. We could finish up in lonely isolated areas. We could be working with people who were violent due to their drug and alcohol use. And any children we might have could be put at great risk.

I needn't have worried about Bev's response. I cried with joy when I read it: 'I wouldn't want anything else in life but to be your wife and to be with you in any work you might do. Besides, I think my work out at the Aboriginal reserve has been preparing me for something special. And I loved it on occasions when you were out there working with me.' She included the words from a Christian hymn as part of her reply, affirming that she was committed to being with me however hard and dangerous our Christian work might be.

> Down in the valley with my Saviour I would go
> Where the storms are sweeping and the dark waters flow
> With His hand to lead me I will never, never fear
> Dangers cannot fright me if my Lord is near. (And you!)

I could hardly wait to head up to Bev. Exams came and went, and I surprised myself by continuing to get good marks. But although I was thoroughly enjoying college life and especially work experience, time was really dragging.

Then all of a sudden I hitchhiked up to St George, and before I knew it 24 December had arrived. That Christmas Eve, Bev and I drove to the banks of the Balonne. To outsiders it may not have appeared to be very romantic, but to the two of us, and especially to me, it was the most romantic spot on earth.

It would have been even more nostalgic to sit in my FC ute, instead we were in Bev's parents' Mini Minor van, which was used at the family supermarket. But the vehicle didn't really matter; the important thing was that we were at 'The swimming hole' on the Balonne, the place where I had first visualised Bev as a rose in the desert, standing out as a dark-haired, fair-complexioned beauty in the sunburnt Queensland countryside, alongside other ladies who faded significantly in comparison to her. This was where I'd seen something very special in Bev, and where for me it really was love at first sight. It hadn't taken us long to believe we were meant for each other, and now we were absolutely certain.

We giggled a bit at the formality of my proposal—especially when Bev passed me the engagement ring that she had purchased, having paid it off at a local jewellery shop.

'Darling,' I said, 'I am head over heels in love with you, and I believe that we are meant for each other and that it is God's will for us to be married. Will you marry me?'

'Of course I will,' Bev answered in her matter-of-fact way. 'I feel the same way. I can't wait to be doing Christian work with you.'

~

We were eager to tell those at home the news. It was well into the evening, about nine, but because it was Christmas Eve, Bev's parents were still up, plus her sisters Sherril and Julianne. They were waiting for the service at the Anglican church, starting at eleven.

Bev was now eighteen. Her oldest sister Glenis, twenty, had been married during the year and was living in Brisbane. Their brother Eric, twenty-one, was married and living away also. Sherril, sixteen, and Julianne, four, lived at home. Ted, twenty-four, still lived at home but was out with mates.

Sherril was very excited when we made the announcement, having been very much part of my life and Eddie's from when we'd first arrived in St George. Julianne was caught up in the excitement of the moment without understanding what was going on, although she was enthralled by Bev's engagement ring. Mr Beaton was pretty formal in his congratulations, not expressing much emotion, while his wife was clearly worried.

Mrs Beaton was very close to Bev, who had been quite sick as a young child, and was terrified of losing her. While we hadn't set a date yet, in her mind it was a fait accompli—and if Bev and I lived and worked anywhere other than Queensland, anywhere away from home, it might as well be on the other side of the world. Her Beverley would be lost.

The following day we told Ted, Eric and Glenis the news. Ted was warm and eloquent in his congratulations, while Eric was fairly inexpressive and matter-of-fact, a bit like his dad. Glenis was over the moon, however. She knew me well, having bonded closely with me while I was living in St George. I think she was also glad to see Bev moving away from home and becoming independent as she had.

Needless to say, our Christian friends in St George were thrilled that Bev and I had finally taken the step that to them was obvious: being formally and openly committed to each other and God for Christian service. Our Bible discussion group at the Fletchers' house held a great informal engagement party. Jack Evans and Stan Fletcher prayed over us, asking for God's blessing and guidance for our future together. Bev's girlfriends in the group—especially Desley Fletcher, Lyn Holland and Elaine Campbell—were very excited for her and so glad that we were the first couple from their group who would be joining together in Christian work.

~

During my final year at college, I got regular work experience at the Melbourne City Mission Men's Centre in North Melbourne. It was a drop-in centre for homeless people, mostly alcoholics and mostly men; despite its name, women sometimes attended. Before there were social workers and welfare workers in the community generally, City Missions were the referral centres for welfare needs in each Australian capital city. Seven days a week, the centre gave out a free breakfast, clothing and toiletries, as well as a devotional address. A church service was conducted over breakfast every Sunday by a different church. MBI students were rostered to assist there every Saturday, and we were charged with giving the devotional address—pity the people we practised on!

The mission superintendent, Reverend Ron Barnes, visited MBI during my second year and challenged students to consider work among homeless people as a local mission option after graduation. Together with prison work, this resonated with me very strongly. I discussed it with Ron, and towards the end of the year he put a proposition to me. The missioner or manager of the City Mission Men's Centre was due to retire, and the mission was offering me the position of assistant to the missioner on six months' probation beginning January 1967. If my probationary period was satisfactory, the current missioner would retire and I would be appointed in his place. After much prayer and consideration, and long-distance discussion with Bev, I accepted the offer.

At the end of the year, just one task remained: graduate from the Melbourne Bible Institute. It still seemed very surreal. From atheism to Christianity. From backwoods to Bible college. From primary school education to tertiary education. All accomplished in under three years.

The grandiose graduation ceremony was held in the ornate Melbourne Town Hall on Monday, 28 November 1966. There must have been a thousand friends and relatives present—but sadly none of my relatives or friends, except one, was able to be there: Desley Fletcher, Bev's best friend and Stan's daughter, who had been attending MBI that year. Even though she wasn't due to graduate until the following year, she stayed behind for my ceremony, and I was thrilled. She not only represented Bev but the entire great group from St George who were responsible for pointing me in the direction that turned my life around.

My graduation was immensely rewarding and inspiring. Whatever walk of life the other seventy-two graduates had come from, we were all equal. I now had a clear vision and a solid path for my future. More than that, I had a life partner to share it with. Bring on our marriage! The date had been set for 20 May the following year, 1967.

~

Over Christmas I went to Eildon to catch up with Mum and my siblings—and Prince, who had settled in very well with the family. Then, on 3 January, I commenced my live-in role as assistant to the missioner.

Heckle and Jeckle, the famous first pair of Bill's pet magpies, sitting on Bill's cap. Over sixty years later, the Birdman again has a pair of magpies by that name.

Bill's stepfather Victor Sutcliffe Senior served during World War I in the Australian Army and during World War II in the Australian Air Force.

Des Wood (left) with a nineteen-year-old Bill Sutcliffe. Des was a great mentor to Bill, just as his father Charlie had been before him.

Bill as a twenty-year-old sawyer in the Marouga Sawmill, Queensland. Manager Stan Fletcher had a significant impact on Bill's life.

Bill's seventeen-year-old brother Eddie working in the Marouga Sawmill. Although slightly built, he was very strong and resilient.

Bill with his first car, his pride and joy, an Austin A40 with illuminated wings that protruded to give turning signals.

Bill's beautiful Scotch Collie dog Prince. A prize-winning show dog, he travelled with Bill and Eddie and later was a great watchdog for Bill's mother and family.

Bill and Bev's wedding party, from left to right: at the back, Bill Beaton (Bev's Dad); in the middle, Kathleen Beaton (Bev's mum), Max and Desley Fletcher, Eddie Sutcliffe, Sherril Beaton (Bev's sister), Bill and Bev, and Lillian Smith (Bill's mum); at the front, flower girl Julianne Beaton (Bev's sister).

Some of the men from the Melbourne City Mission Men's Centre rehabilitation program, joining Bill, Bev and their young kids on a special occasion.

Bill greeting men as they are about to enter the Melbourne City Mission for breakfast, a shave, and fresh clothing. Some two hundred people came to the centre on a daily basis.

Men from the Melbourne City Mission enjoying carpet bowls. Bev is in the left foreground, Bill squatting opposite her.

(Inset) Bill as a student at the Melbourne Bible Institute.

A well-earned rest and ice-cream for Bill from his daughter Pamela after he ran 27 laps—or 162 kilometres—around Lake Wendouree to raise money for the Ballarat Children's Home.

Bill training for a failed attempt at the World Non-Stop Running Record; his badly blistered feet forced him to stop.

From left: David Searle, Bill Sutcliffe and Ivan Sutcliffe (Bill's brother) completing a 79-kilometre sponsored run from Geelong to Buninyong, in order to purchase computers for a local preschool. David joined the run at the end as a business sponsor.

The Ballarat Town and City Mission Netball team, coached by Bill, after winning the 1977 Grand Final. (Photo courtesy of *The Courier/* ACM)

Part of the 100-strong Ballarat Town and City Mission Awana Youth Club after winning the State Awana Championship.

Sunday School the Shetland pony, trained and driven by Bill with his daughter Christine alongside, entertaining Eureka Street Primary schoolchildren.

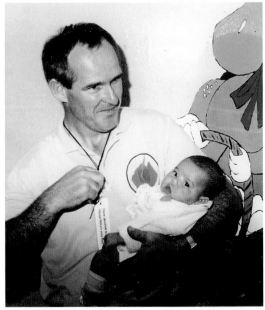

Bill in South Africa in 1979 with Prince Mangosuthu Buthelezi, the traditional prime minister of the Zulu Nation.

Bill holding the child of a female inmate in a prison in Costa Rica, Central America.

Bill outside the Federal Prison Camp at Maxwell, Montgomery, in the US, where Chuck Colson had been incarcerated.

Bill assisting his father-in-law Bill Beaton to climb out of a mine shaft that they had sunk together, with Bill's sons David and Paul.

The relocatable house placed on Genesis in Buninyong to accommodate people in need, including ex-prisoners.

The house that Bill, Bev and their family, with volunteers, ultimately built on their property.

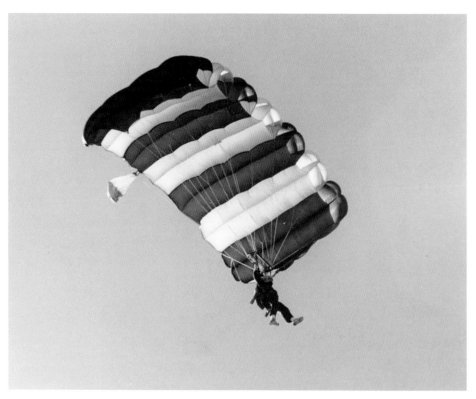

The inaugural solo parachute jump Bill made to celebrate his fiftieth birthday.

Bill arriving in Colac from on high via a tandem parachute jump to commence his time as Minister of Colac Church of Christ.

Bill with the world champion ultramarathon runner Yiannis Kouros at the finish of the Colac Six-Day Race.

Ultramarathon runners celebrating the Six-Day Race. Bill is second from the right, and on his left is the legendary Cliffy Young.

Bill, as president of the Six–Day Race, displaying the honour board beside the famous Cliffy Young gumboot.

Bill with Lord Mayor of Melbourne John So, having run from Ballarat to Melbourne to invite Melbournians to attend the famous Ballarat Begonia Festival.

Bill with Bev and their children at his graduation from Deakin University. From left to right: at the back, Paul, David, Bill, Bev, Mark and Sara; at the front, Angela, Pamela and Christine.

Bill's graduation from Deakin University. Bev is quite rightly helping to hold his BA Literature Major Certificate—she had helped him with his writing years before.

Bill with his Graduation Certificate from the University of Ballarat.

Bill in front of the Colac Church of Christ prior to running in the Six-Day Race. (Photo courtesy of the Warrnambool *Standard*)

Bill walking with Ballarat Specialist School students in the beautiful Otway Ranges.

Bill with his biological father, Bob Turner.

Bill's biological siblings, from left to right: at the back, Lila, Eddie, Bill and Norma; at the front, Val, Gladys, Denice, Jeannie and Ivan.

The Sutcliffe family on Genesis, from left to right: at the back, Sara, Angela, Christine and Pamela; in the middle, Mark, David, family friend Chuck, and Paul; at the front, Bill and Bev.

Bill with his mother, Lillian Smith.

Bill challenging his mother to a walking-frame race. The twinkle in her eye suggests she was going to take him on!

Bev and Bill.

My experience at the City Mission Men's Centre was disconcerting from the beginning. The centre was situated on the corner of Arden and Abbotsford streets, North Melbourne, just a torpedo punt kick from the North Melbourne football ground. The double-storied building was formerly the Prince of Wales Hotel. It was ironic that the premise was now being used to assist a great many who had been badly affected by alcohol. Two hundred plus homeless men and an occasional woman would arrive daily for breakfast, then have a shave, a change of clothes and a general clean-up before hitting the streets again.

It was difficult for me as a 23-year-old to walk in the shoes of the seventy-year-old missioner. I had to be careful, though, that I wasn't a smart aleck or full of myself and unteachable. Coming from a relatively sheltered background, he'd been unused to dealing with drunks and alcoholics. He had great trouble handling problematic people dropping in off the streets, and there were plenty of them. His main way of dealing with difficult people was to ban them from the centre or from having breakfast—to put their name in a Black Book. However, he didn't have a book big enough! I tried to reason with him about the futility of some of these bans, suggesting that the disruptiveness could be managed in a different way. For example, even if we had to ban a disruptive person from devotions, at least we could send them away with something to eat and welcome them back the next day to start afresh. I thought that was a Christian principle, but he disagreed.

I couldn't rock the boat too much, conscious that my wedding was coming up and that Bev was looking forward to the challenge of being involved in the drop-in centre. Bev did all the wedding planning, and I worked at the centre until a week before the ceremony. My probationary period was to continue for two months after our honeymoon.

I didn't have a car and was grateful that a fellow MBI student gave me a ride all the way to a service station in Moonie. I only had to hitchhike a hundred miles or so to St George. It was a hot and steamy day, but passing vehicles were so scarce that I wasn't game to go into the servo for a drink in case I missed a ride. I stood on the roadside for an inordinate amount of time in the heat, and a good Samaritan brought me out a cold drink.

Then an embarrassing thing happened. A car coming from the direction of St George pulled up—it was my soon to be parents-in-law, heading to Toowoomba to collect Bev's grandmother for the wedding. They were horrified to find their soon to be son-in-law hitchhiking up to marry their daughter. Shortly afterwards, Bev received a phone call. Her parents asked her to drive to Moonie and pick me up—just a 200-mile round trip!

My best mate and brother Eddie was to be my best man, travelling up and back with Mum and Ellis. Unfortunately, with such a big family and such a small budget, seven of my brothers and sisters ranging from just six years of age couldn't come to the wedding, and the older ones had to look after the younger. Good mates that I had met at MBI came up too. True to tradition, the night before the wedding I stayed away from Bev and had a bucks' night at a friend's house. As a Christian, and because my background was so marred by alcohol, I'd decided with Bev that there wouldn't be any alcohol at my bucks' night or at our wedding. The bucks' night was great fun nevertheless. My MBI mates fitted right in with Ellis,

Eddie, and my friends from the youth group and National Fitness Club. All sorts of tales were told about me in college and some of my pranks there.

Another tradition would have it that you can't have a bucks' night without a prank on the groom. I madly sprinted around the backyard trying to evade capture, then got into some solid tackles and frenzied wrestles. When they finally subdued me, they tied me to the clothesline with just my briefs on. Could have been worse—could have been with nothing on! It was a chilly autumn evening, but it could have been midwinter. Then came the dobs of shaving cream, then toilet paper stuck to the cream. When the wind rose, I was flapping like a helicopter rotor and thought I would take off, clothesline and all! In the end my assailants only left me there for half an hour or so, after Eddie told them they couldn't allow me to finish up with pneumonia on my honeymoon.

～

Our wedding was a wonderful celebration of two people from very different backgrounds coming together to complement each other's lives with their different gifts and talents. The ceremony was conducted in the local Church of England, where Bev and her family attended and she had taught Sunday school. The reception was held in the Civic Hall and catered for professionally. A magnificent roast dinner was served to some eighty guests representing Bev's family and mine as well as friends from the Church Youth Group and National Fitness Club and of course MBI. Mrs Fletcher, Desley's mother, baked, iced and decorated a beautiful twin-tiered wedding cake with flowers and bows and bells.

I'm sure not everyone understood or readily accepted our decision to have a dry reception. Equally, for some guests the Christian speeches must have seemed like a foreign language.

It rained heavily throughout the night as we travelled towards Brisbane for our honeymoon. We stayed in the beautiful seaside resort of Redcliffe. Other than relaxing together and enjoying the scenery, and especially each other, our highlight was a visit to the Brisbane City Mission in Fortitude Valley.

Reverend Clarrie Trudgian was the superintendent, a remarkable man. He had won a Military Cross on the Western Front in 1918. An ordained Churches of Christ minister and welfare worker, he had been appointed superintendent in 1939, towards the end of the Great Depression. He'd immediately started to reform and expand the mission. Its motto then was 'To care for the disadvantaged and poor', and in the beginning the bulk of the work was soup kitchens along with food and clothing handouts. Clarrie didn't accept a salary for the first ten years; he sold flowers to obtain an income and believed the Lord would provide.

I'd contacted Clarrie to make an appointment for me and Bev to visit the mission, which was named Trudgian House. He asked me if we could visit when the staff were providing a free breakfast for homeless people and others in need, and if I could give a devotional talk over the meal. I was happy to oblige. That morning, Bev and I trudged up a set of stairs to the first floor of the mission where breakfast was being served, and the opening remarks of my devotion were, 'After trudging up the stairs to get here, I can understand why this building is called Trudgian House!' The guests had a laugh, and Clarrie took it in good humour also.

While Bev and I were still on our honeymoon, the minister of the West Melbourne Baptist Church contacted us and offered us the use of their church manse rent-free. It was a sizeable house in which to start out our married life: three bedrooms, a large lounge room, a spacious kitchen, laundry, bathroom and office, and a big front room where a church service was held every Sunday morning. We were welcome to use it, providing that we could cope with it being on an island!

'An island?' I asked incredulously. 'In the heart of Melbourne?'

'Yes,' he said, 'it was created a few decades ago when the road system through West Melbourne was being reconfigured. This left a triangle of three roads with one house and a vacant block in the middle. The house contained the West Melbourne Baptist Church, and the government of the day decided not to compulsorily acquire it. A service station was built on the vacant block. What do you think?'

My humour cut in. 'I get the picture. So instead of water lapping the island and noisy boats circling it, we'll just have constant trucks and cars?'

'Yes, but you forgot the service station, Bill. That might be worse than crocodiles infesting a normal island. Not trying to turn you off, just painting an honest picture!'

Perhaps it should have been called 'The Island Church'. I told him I was sure we could cope with it, but I would need to put it past Bev.

Like me, she had stars in her eyes and excitement in her heart for what lay ahead. 'Yes, we should take the manse,' she said. 'After all, it's rent-free—it's God providing our need.'

From Redcliffe we drove back to St George and said our fare-wells. Then we flew to Melbourne and took up residence in the manse, not far from the Melbourne City Mission Men's Centre where I would be continuing my probationary period. And we were just a stone's throw from the famous Queen Victoria Market.

The Melbourne mid-winter weather was a shock for Bev, coming from warm, outback Queensland. Some people commented that they only recognised her because of her green coat, which she never seemed to take off. Like my moving from the country to the city for the first time at MBI, there was not just one, but many shocks for Bev. But as I had proved, endurance is proportionate to commitment, and Bev had committed herself to go down into the valleys with me as well as to the mountain tops—she would get through with flying colours.

12

Into the fray

I had a week to settle into the manse with Bev, then I set off back to work at the centre. It was so good to be there again. Visiting the Brisbane City Mission had reinforced my belief that my heart was with the disenfranchised and that I was suited for this work. The missioner and his volunteers were very welcoming on my return, keen to know how my wedding had gone and to get feedback on my visit to the mission in Brisbane. They also got a good laugh out of the account of Bev and I trudging up the stairs of Trudgian House! They were keen to meet Bev, who I had talked up so much.

Nothing had changed at the centre, though. On my very first day back, the missioner stopped a group of men from entering the building for breakfast, stating that they were trouble-makers and couldn't come in—that they were in the Black Book. The men looked cold and hungry, so I quietly told them to call in at the Hawke Street Baptist Manse and my wife would give them something to eat. Unfortunately I had no way of informing Bev of this, so I just hoped for the best. She told me later that she was horrified when she opened the front door and found a group of unkempt men, reeking of alcohol and saying, 'Bill told us you'll give us some food!' She quickly closed the door and left them standing on the front porch. Then she made some sandwiches, opened the door slightly, and passed the plate out the door to them. That was the start of many new, enlightening, frightening experiences for Bev.

I became increasing concerned about the Black Book philosophy and found it hard to keep quiet about it. I understood that there had to be some discipline, but for it to be indefinite seemed like a life sentence for a minor or moderate crime. Consequently I found myself at cross-purposes with the missioner. The straw that broke the camel's back for me came when I was standing alongside the missioner one morning as people were pouring in for breakfast. As I said, 'Welcome, buddy,' to a guy trying to brush past me, the missioner put his hand in front of him like a mechanical arm in a carpark suddenly coming down. Then he said something to me that shocked me and really got my hackles up. 'Bill, don't cast your pearls before swine. He's in the Black Book.'

I couldn't get it off my mind during the mini-sermon delivered by the missioner, or while the homeless people were eating breakfast, or while they were coming into the clothing room to receive free garments. After they had lined up to have a shave, I could hold my tongue no longer. When the last man had left the mission, and the volunteers were sitting down having a cuppa, I took the missioner aside to express my concern.

I started positively. 'I need to tell you how much I am impressed with the service that is provided here and the tremendous work that you and the volunteers are doing, but something is bothering me. As a Christian like you are, I was quite shocked to hear you say earlier this morning in reference to one of the guys, "Don't cast your pearls before swine."' He went red in the face and opened his mouth to say something, but I said, 'If I could just briefly finish, please. I was reading the Bible recently, the part where Jesus was criticised by religious people for eating and drinking with undesirable people, and he replied, "It's not those who are well who need a doctor, but those who are sick."'

He exploded. 'How dare you, you young upstart! You've been a Christian for ten minutes and worked here for five, and you've probably never read the Bible, yet you're telling me what Jesus said and how to do my job!'

I felt guilty for a moment, but then I remembered Powder-Monkey Jimmy's words, 'You're no one's superior but anyone's equal,' and was about to enter the fray again.

The missioner didn't allow me to speak. 'Get out of my sight, you proud, arrogant, would-be mission worker. Do you realise you're on probation here? I'll be making a full report of this incident to the superintendent.'

Not unexpectedly, my probationary period was found to be unsatisfactory, so I had to leave. Strange as it may seem, I was convinced that I was still meant to have the role of missioner there. Some words had come to my mind from the Bible: 'I have set an open door before you and no man can shut it.' I believed that the tables would be turned in due course.

∼

It was late July 1967. Bev and I had only been married two months, and here I was out of work. She was expecting our first child and understandably anxious. We were fortunate to have a rent-free roof over our heads, though, and an assurance from the Baptist church that we were welcome to stay as long as necessary. Fellow students from Bible college, hearing of our plight, rounded up some groceries for us and assisted us greatly. Throughout all this I was convinced that things were going to work out for the better. If the worst came to the worst, Bev could go home to her parents for a few weeks until things were sorted out. She was very homesick, and her mum was missing her terribly and would have loved to have her back for a while.

I'd been away from the mission for a couple of weeks when an idea came out of left field: I considered becoming a nurse. Male nursing was still in its infancy, but I could see how the experience would be an excellent asset when working with homeless people, so I applied to do a course at the Royal Melbourne Hospital. The medical superintendent, Dr Jamieson, had been a missionary, and he was keen for me to train as a nurse, believing as I did that the experience would be useful for me.

The only setback was that the hospital required an assurance I would stay on for a reasonable amount of time after my training. I was so convinced that I was going back to the mission that I couldn't give that assurance. Dr Jamieson was very understanding and gave me another option: a position was soon to become available for a medical orderly in charge of the male observation ward in casualty. The role consisted mainly of observing casualty intakes, which involved tasks such as taking their temperature, pulse rate and blood pressure. 'Gain a bit of experience in overall hospital work first as a general orderly,

Bill, then I can arrange for you to have some specific training for the observation ward and you can take up the role.'

It didn't take long for me to be trained and orientated into the role. The observations that needed to be made were pretty basic, but they were vital, especially in the casualty ward. If patients weren't seriously injured but had lost consciousness, they had to be observed for a minimum of four hours. Shining a small torchlight on eye pupils to see if they were enlarged could determine if there was possibly a serious head injury.

One of the more unpleasant tasks was to go out to an ambulance and be a witness as a doctor certified somebody as dead on arrival. Accident victims were often a terrible sight.

Casualty could be a dangerous place. Head injuries and alcohol sometimes caused considerable volatility and associated physical violence. Ironically, because of that I felt very much at home in my new job, which unfortunately meant I was constantly reminded of the violence caused in my childhood by alcohol.

Working in casualty was an invaluable experience neverthe-less—an eye-opening one. I saw the men from the mission in a much rawer way. Many of them had been struck by vehicles or assaulted by people who hatefully called them 'deros', 'deadbeats' and 'no-hopers'. It made my blood boil for them to be judged so harshly and ignorantly. In the brief period that I'd got to know some of them, I had learnt that there was a former doctor and a former test cricketer among their ranks, people from all walks of life. 'There but for the grace of God go I.' Most of them were chronic alcoholics, and some provided an interesting perspective on the slang term 'demon drink'—they claimed to have been directed by the Devil to walk against red lights, or to step in front of cars, or to jump off bridges. It was always suicidal acts that they were asked to do, never life-saving ones. I began to see these men as more fragile and vulnerable than I ever had before.

~

On the twenty-third of February 1968, our first child, David John, was born.

When Bev's doctor had told her she was pregnant, I'd been ecstatic and thankful—to Bev and to God. I was overcome with emotion. I had read in the Bible that 'Children are a blessing from the Lord', and I felt ever so blessed. This was the greatest coming of age there could have been for me: the prospect of parenthood, of being a father, of being a good one. The image of the father I had, yet didn't know, flooded my mind. I was twenty-five and hadn't seen him for over twenty-three years. There were tears of joy and sorrow.

Things progressed reasonably well until the seventh-month mark, when Bev's blood pressure started to get dangerously high. Six weeks before the due date, she was admitted to the Queen Victoria Hospital with pre-eclampsia. She had a Bible at her bedside and was heavily sedated. At one point she asked if a nurse could read a comforting Psalm to her, and it transpired that the nurse had graduated from Bible college with me!

David was induced urgently, then whisked away and placed in a humidicrib, while Bev was very ill and had to stay in an intensive-care room. She was only wheeled around to see her firstborn after two days, and then not allowed to hold him. Fortunately I was able to see and bottle-feed David daily, thanks to my college associate making allowances. He was a beautiful placid baby with an olive complexion and big dark winsome eyes.

Bev had to remain in hospital for two weeks, and I spent another two at home with her before returning to work at the hospital. Bev and David were both doing well, and one of the Baptist ladies offered to keep an eye on them and do what she could to help. I went back to work floating on cloud nine. Whenever a staff member said, 'Congratulations, Bill, I hear you've become a father,' my chest just about burst with pride, and I hastened to reply, 'But Bev did all the hard work, and it was difficult for her.'

~

All was pretty well with the world. Then, out of the blue, my sister Val informed me that she had tracked down our father. She'd placed advertisements in Melbourne newspapers to try and locate him, they'd been fruitful, and she had arranged for us to meet him.

The thought of being in contact with him was very strange to me. I had been under two years of age when my parents separated—after he had thrown a knife at my mother and hit me instead, causing me to lose an eye—he hadn't seen me for twenty-four years, let alone said sorry or as much as sent a Christmas or birthday card. He was a stranger to me.

We were to meet in the home of his partner Lily. It was interesting, I thought, that she shared her first name with our mother.

Val, Bev and I, with David in a carry basket, found ourselves crowded into a tiny bedsitter. There weren't enough chairs for us in the lounge room, so Bev and the baby sat on the end of the bed with the door open.

If you had been a fly on the wall, you would have observed the weirdest meeting. A married daughter desperate to see her father after a 24-year separation. A son, a victim of horrific domestic violence at his father's hands, once very bitter and non-forgiving, now a changed person. A father totally at sea, not knowing what to say and not saying anything.

In the background the TV was screening a comedy of all things, Graham Kennedy and Bert Newton on *In Melbourne Tonight*. I was trying to make polite conversation with the man in front of me called my father, asking what he did by way of work, and did he follow the footy? Yes, he was a keen Carlton supporter, and was a fitter and turner by trade.

Val was talking quickly, undoubtedly releasing nervous tension. 'Are there any other children, half brothers or sisters?'

'No,' he said.

Then he asked me if he could speak to me privately. There was no such thing as privacy in such a small space; although he took me into a corner, everyone could hear what he said. 'I want you to change you surname back to mine and drop your religion.'

I was shocked, flabbergasted, speechless. When I glanced at Bev, her body language said it all. She was stunned.

I regained my composure. 'That's impossible. I've grown up with my brothers and sisters with the same name, so I'd be betraying them to change my name from theirs now. And as far as changing my religion, there is no chance of that. Christianity took me from hatred and bitterness and non-forgiveness to love and peace and forgiveness. The only reason I'm here meeting you, and prepared to be reconciled with you, is my religion.'

My father shook his head, mumbled something and walked back to his chair, and he didn't speak to me again that day.

It was different for Val, who had a married name. She tried to reason with him but in vain. Finally we all just had to leave.

After this very emotional meeting with my father, I had much cause to consider the place and value of religion in my life. Christianity—or, as I saw it, my relationship with Jesus—was the greatest and deepest resource I had. As I'd tried to tell Dad, I wouldn't have been meeting with him if it hadn't been for the miracle of being enabled to forgive. I reflected on the incredible love and support that the Catholic Wood family in Wycheproof had given me, and the amazing acceptance, tolerance and guidance that the Christians in St George had given me also. These experiences proved to me that through religion I had a destiny—to see the best in the blackest sheep and to help them recognise their worth as others had done for me. That's why I had loved working at the mission.

~

Before long, Bev and I had taken a recovering alcoholic into our home. He had spent many years in prison. My only request was that he be sober and want to do something positive with his life, and we would assist him with that. But he nearly drove Bev mad: he called her 'Madam' and would always spread a newspaper over the table before eating a meal. He moved on after a couple of months.

Then the Baptist minister asked us if we could take an alcoholic man into our home and assist him. The minister assured us that this man had become a Christian, was a real gentleman, and was absolutely committed to turning his life around. We took him in.

At first it seemed the minister was correct. This man was a former medical student with a dignified demeanour, and he fitted in like one of the family—when he was sober!

The day came when he got back on the drink. I was at work when he turned up at the manse and banged on our front door, swearing and demanding to be let in. Bev had never seen him that way before and was terrified. Having a baby in the house, she quickly locked all the doors and windows, then pretended not to be home. The man went around the house looking for signs that someone was there, all the time yelling abuse and demanding to be let in. The manse had no phone and no neighbours, so Bev stayed hidden in the bedroom with David. That was until she heard a crash and realised the man had smashed the window to his room. He climbed in and began breaking every bit of furniture as he cursed and swore. Bev got on her knees and prayed, then picked up a dustpan and brush, walked quietly to his room and said, 'This is a disgraceful mess. Clean it up!' With that he started to cry and apologise, and to clean up his room. He didn't stay long after that.

It never ceased to amaze me how Bev coped. She came from a relatively sheltered and insular background, yet she was incredibly accepting and brave—in fact, heroic. She had just turned twenty-one and, in the space of a little over a year, had got married, left her close-knit family in a quiet Queensland town, and moved to a seedy, populous suburb of Melbourne, frequented by many noisy and sometimes violent alcoholics. Within that same timeframe she'd given birth to her first child prematurely, and after the difficult pregnancy and birth, she was sharing her first marital home and her newborn baby with some of those alcoholics.

I was incredibly naive and perhaps exercising a blind faith that all would be well. It was relatively easy for me because this world was my background, while for Bev it was a frightening new frontier. I'm sure she was reflecting her parents' outback Queensland 'just get on with it' spirit—their first marital home had been a tent. But more so, she had made an absolute spiritual commitment before marriage that she was prepared to go down in the valleys as well as to the mountain tops.

~

Among the men I had originally directed to our house for a feed were the brothers Jim and Bill Bentley. They continued to call at the manse daily for food, and before long they started arriving in the middle of the night and camping in a small shed out the back. They would be perpetually drunk, inevitably having a stash of alcohol that would keep them supplied all night, and being noisy and boisterous all night long as well.

Late one dark, cold night under a bridge in West Melbourne, I had come across Jim while I was searching for homeless men in abandoned houses and under bridges. As I shone my torch beneath a particular bridge, there he was, a saveloy in his mouth. He was gripping it with his teeth like his life depended on it. To my amazement, a rat was hanging on to the other end!

In my torchlight the animal relinquished the sausage and scampered away. Not Jim, though. He had won the tug of war and was determined to eat the saveloy—and eat it he did, despite my intrusion. 'Hey, what the bloody hell are you doin' in my house?' he roared. 'Are you a John Hop?'

'Mate, I came for a meal. I thought you were going to let the rat have it all!'

'Well you can't have any—there's hardly enough for me!' he said as he slurped the last bit down. 'Who are you, anyway?'

'I'm One-Eyed Billy,' I said, whipping out my artificial eye and holding it towards him. 'I'm here to keep an eye on you.'

'*Whaaaat?* I like your style. Make yourself at home.'

Jim was to become a central character in our family as well as in our Christian work. The youngest of ten sons, he was meant to be named James Tenthson, but when his inebriated father had gone to register his name with very slurred speech, the registrar clerk had thought it was 'Tennyson'.

Although Jim visited us regularly and started to fit in with our household, his brother Bill took a long time to come in through the front door. Each day he would sit on the porch and wait for Bev to bring him sandwiches. She was amazing—each day she moved the chair Bill would sit on closer to the door, until one day she left the door open and put the chair just inside. At first he didn't take the bait and didn't stay around for sandwiches, but the next time hunger and perhaps greater inebriation caused him to throw caution to the wind—he sat inside the house! Bev's love and perseverance had triumphed.

Socks was another one of those from the Black Book who had come over for a feed. A tall, gangly man, probably in his late thirties, he was a chronic alcoholic. Had Bev known the reason he was homeless, she may have been decidedly nervous.

One day Socks fell and hit his head, losing consciousness on a city street. An ambulance brought him to the Royal Melbourne

Hospital, where he was found to have no major injuries but needed to spend four hours in casualty to ensure there were no delayed effects. I happened to be working a shift, and Socks talked away to me like I was his long-lost brother, maybe because of the heavy knock he had sustained! It was midweek, and the casualty intake was relatively quiet. In between looking after other patients and an occasional intake, I listened as Socks told me his story.

In the late 1950s when 6 p.m. closing was the law in hotels, Socks would partake in 'the six o'clock swill'. It was a literal swill: publicans tiled the walls around the bar so that the splashed beer could be washed off more readily.

One fateful night Socks was intent on having his fill of alcohol before six, when a barmaid dared to tell him that he'd had enough. He reached over for yet another drink and she pushed his hand away, then went to pick up the remaining glasses. He swore and leant over the bar to grab one from her. With that, she leant towards him and tried to push him off the bar. In Socks's words: 'I was so angry and so desperate for a drink, I didn't think—I hit her. She fell down behind the bar. She was unconscious. Someone called out, "You've killed her." Some men tried to stop me, but I ran out and kept running. I ran a couple of states away to Victoria.

'Things had been going bad before this—I'd been hitting the slops more and more—and then I really went downhill. I was a murderer on the run, forever on edge, always looking over my shoulder. Alcohol was my only escape. I couldn't hold down a job. I was never sober enough. Now I had no job, no money, and no hope. I was wandering aimlessly around the streets, from handout place to handout place, from dosshouse to dosshouse. At least I didn't stand out in the overcoat brigade.

'But eventually I tried to face up to my crime. I decided to visit the pub, tell them I was the bloke who'd killed the barmaid, and ask them to call the police. I don't know how I managed to make it there. The closer I got, the guiltier I felt, the more scared I was, the more I drank. I was trembling as I staggered into the hotel. *Wait!* I thought. *I can't believe it. Am I dreaming? That woman behind the bar is her! She's still alive.* I was numb. I stumbled out, without saying a word, and went back to skid row.'

~

I had absolutely loved my brief time at the mission and remained quite convinced that I was meant to be there. I was making frequent contact with homeless people in the casualty ward, and many of them were coming to our home. Had I thrown away the opportunity of a lifetime to be a nurse? All I could do was write to the superintendent of the mission, the Reverend Ron Barnes, outlining all the experience I had gained while I'd been away. I told him that although I couldn't go to the men at the mission, they had come to me. Amazingly, the superintendent reversed the original decision: he retired the incumbent Missioner and appointed me. I was twenty-six years of age, and Bev was just twenty-two. Everything had indeed worked together for the good.

In February 1969, before we moved out of the manse, our second child was born. Paul Timothy was premature also, because once again Bev had high blood pressure. I had booked her into the

Vaucluse private hospital on 12 February, and Paul was induced at 11 a.m. He was born with the blondest hair you could imagine and the loudest cry. The nurses all said he would be a singer! David was placid and quiet, while Paul was noisy and full of energy and mischief, keeping Bev on her toes when I was busy at work.

Just after Paul was born, in 1969, we shifted into a flat above the Men's Centre. During the year, students from MBI continued to come to the centre for work experience. One of them was Chuck Mendenhall, a former American Marine who had served in the Korean War. Chuck had migrated to Australia and become an Australian Citizen. He really took a shine to the work and Bev and me, as we did to him. After his term's assignment at the centre was finished, he asked if he could come back as a volunteer. We were happy to have him. He had also done some interesting work in California—as a guide at the famous Knott's Berry Farm tourist attraction, then as a courier, making deliveries to Disneyland, Graceland (the home of Elvis Presley) as well as to John Wayne's residence. He met him a number of times.

The second storey in what had been the Prince of Wales Hotel was now being used to assist alcoholics to obtain sobriety! There were steep stairs leading up to it, and because Paul was soon a very active baby, we were worried about his safety. Mischievous child that he was, we were also concerned that he would get David involved. We got our maintenance man to put bars on the windows and as much protection around for our children as possible. Despite that, we were still periodically plagued by thoughts that perhaps we were putting our children at great risk in such an environment.

Later in the year, when Paul had been crawling for a while and was starting to walk, Bev's parents drove all the way from St George to visit us. It was an epic journey for them, especially as they'd never driven that far before, but they were feeling very excited, and so was Bev. They hadn't seen her since she'd moved away, and this would be their first time meeting their new grandchildren.

My parents-in-law arrived in North Melbourne via the new Tullamarine Freeway. Bev's dad maintained that he and his wife had officially opened the freeway by being the first people to drive on it other than workmen. The truth was, they inadvertently drove around a barrier to get onto it. My father-in-law must have thought the freeway was a godsend—he hated heavy traffic at the best of times and had the road to himself.

When they were nearly at the mission, Bev's dad stopped to ask a pedestrian for directions. 'I'll give you directions, mate,' he said, 'but for a fee.' He reluctantly gave him $5. Pointing just down the road, the man said, 'That's the mission there.' It was only a block away. Bev's dad noticed him at the mission the following day, and he wasn't making eye contact!

Bev's parents stayed with us for a week. They were horrified by the two hundred or so dishevelled men, many drunk and aggressive, who shuffled into the mission every day for food, clothing and toiletries. They were understandably concerned not just for their grandchildren's safety but for Bev's also. The three Beaumont children had been abducted from an Adelaide beach in 1966, my last year at Bible college, and the terrifying incident was still fresh in people's minds.

There was a large former alcohol cellar on the ground floor that we used as a clothing storeroom. When I took my father-in-law down there to show him around, he almost turned white and said matter-of-factly, 'Do you realise this old cellar has a trapdoor out onto the street? This would be an ideal place to abduct children from!'

I was speechless for a moment. 'You're right, but the trapdoor has been long sealed over by the footpath. And we won't allow the kids to come down here.'

He didn't seem very reassured.

The poor Beatons. The situation didn't endear me to either of them for a long time.

Following this visit, we got word that my mum had privately married a man named Ernie Smith and that they were going to live at her house in Eildon. There were still four children at home, ranging in age from eighteen to eight and needing a solid father figure. Mum was forty-eight, and Ernie fifty-eight. He was a good man overall—not the most social, but quite caring, which was what Mum wanted at that stage of her life.

13

Mission possible

When Bev joined me at the mission, great organiser and caterer that she was, there was a big assembly line of sandwich-making for the free breakfast. Slices of bread were lined up end to end across the long kitchen bench. Butter was melted in a bowl, and a shaving brush used to spread it on the bread. Different individuals were responsible for inserting different sandwich fillings. We were catering for some two hundred people a day. 'Surely we can do better than this,' Bev proffered. 'Something that's less labour-intensive with more and better food. What do you think?'

I remembered a fellow MBI student who had been a pastry cook at the Coles Cafeteria on Bourke Street. Back when I was doing work experience at the mission, he'd asked me what sort of a breakfast they had, and when I'd said, 'Just so, so,' he'd told me about the great variety of leftovers at the cafeteria, suggesting the staff would readily give this food to the mission. I hadn't been in charge then, but now I could try out this idea. I went in to see Robert Coles at the Bourke Street store, and he was very pleased to arrange for the leftovers to be picked up. Later on, he and his uncle Sir Edgar Coles took a keen interest in the drop-in centre. Robert joined the mission's council of management, and Sir Edgar visited the centre periodically to give encouragement and support.

The food from Coles was supplemented by leftovers from the caterers at the famous Melbourne Cricket Ground. They would ring me at a certain point during a football or cricket match when they believed they had no hope of selling much more food, and I would collect whatever was available. Everyone who came to the mission appreciated this food, and from my perspective it was doubly good—I could catch the end of the day's play of footy or cricket.

Another part of our mission's service was providing free clothing. After breakfast the men and an occasional woman would line up at the door of my office, then file in to tell me what items of clothing they needed—usually quite a few. Many of these people slept under bridges or in old vacant houses, so they didn't have fresh linen or a change of clothes.

One such person was Eileen. Sadly, I didn't really get to know her well. She was a chronic alcoholic who pushed a pram around everywhere she went. One reason she did this was to gather up empty bottles to sell, another was to hide full bottles of alcohol, and perhaps the most practical reason was to camouflage her drunken stagger and to keep herself upright.

It was winter. Eileen brought her pram into the office to safeguard her precious cargo and stay on her feet. She was wearing a khaki army overcoat, known as a greatcoat. It was thick and warm and went right down to her ankles—far from being a fashion statement, and far removed from its army days, but serving a very useful purpose.

'How are you, Eileen?' I asked.

'Not bad.'

'What do you need, my dear?'

Her hands did the talking. Taking them off the handle of her pram, she falteringly opened the buttons of her greatcoat. Then, with a sweeping flourish of her arms that nearly caused her to fall, she opened it up and said, 'Everything!'

'You're right, Eileen,' I said, covering up my surprise. She did need everything. She didn't have a stitch of clothing on. She was stark naked! I felt for Eileen then. How humiliating. How discriminatory. Here she was, lined up with many men at a men's centre, being attended to by a male and indirectly forced to expose herself. Maybe it was a demonstration for just that purpose. In any case it worked. I immediately got Bev to look after her, and she catered for her more personally and understandingly than I ever could, and continued to do so.

~

Jim Bentley regularly attended the mission for breakfast and for the Alcoholics Victorious meetings that we had started to offer, a Christian counterpart to Alcoholics Anonymous that had been around since 1948. At this stage Jim was a bender drinker. He could be sober for a long while, then something would trigger him and he would break out and drink for a considerable time. Even when sober he was unusually talkative for a man with his traumatic background, the type who normally bottled things up. And for someone with only a primary school education, he was a remarkably studious and learned person. He had studied the ancient Spartan people extensively and loved sharing his insights with me, and I loved gleaning them. To some extent he had modelled his life on the Spartans, and he'd say to me, 'Bill, they would never lay down their weapons for any reason, be it hunger or danger. That's why I keep going.'

During World War II, Jim had taken on a nerve-racking role with bomb demolitions. He'd served with the Allies in Japan after the atomic bombs were dropped on Hiroshima and Nagasaki. Between 129,000 and 226,000 Japanese people were killed, and Jim used to say, 'If anything could describe the absolute horrors of war, it was the molten, unidentifiable bodies of those thousands of people, mostly civilians.' He also witnessed the release from Japanese torture camps of thousands of Allied prisoners of war, just skin and bone, with almost fleshless faces and tormented, sunken eyes. As well, he heard at first hand almost indescribable horror stories of man's inhumanity to man inflicted on our soldiers in those camps.

Like many Australians who had witnessed what Jim had, he had a strong hatred for the Japanese. One morning after breakfast, I was wandering around in the mission courtyard, engaging with men washing and shaving, when I heard a roaring voice from the direction of the hall. A man was shouting as he came out into the courtyard.

Then I saw him. It was Jim. He was clenching what looked like a pretty innocuous blunt-ended kitchen knife in his left hand. With that arm stretched rigidly forward, he came charging at me. 'You murdering Jap bastard!' he shouted. *'You're dead.'*

I thought he was joking. Grabbing a metal rubbish-bin lid nearby to use as a shield, I laughed and danced around, pretending we were having a sword fight. But to Jim this was no laughing matter—his very angry features and violent demeanour made that clear. He kept lunging at my shield, ramming the knife into it with almost superhuman strength.

Wow! I thought. *That could do so much damage.*

'He's off his head!' someone called out.

'No, he's got the DTs,' someone else said.

'You're gone, you murdering bastard!' Jim screamed. 'This is for my mates!'

'Jesus!' I shouted, a spontaneous, urgent prayer. *'Jesus!'*

Jim stopped in his tracks and came to his senses. I don't think he had any idea what he had just done, and I was so stunned at what had occurred that it didn't register for a while. While sober, Jim would often analyse his behaviour extensively, and when I mentioned the incident to him, he said, 'That's what happens when you get shell-shocked.' I had heard the phrase before but had never seen the ramifications played out so vividly.

~

On other occasions when Jim broke out on alcohol, he would serenade us outside below our upstairs window for hours during the night. Perhaps one night he was celebrating the homecoming of our third child, Christine Anne.

She had been born on 3 March 1970 and hadn't been home from hospital long. We were absolutely delighted to have a daughter, and she was our first child to be born on the due date without being induced. Christine was a beautiful baby with blue eyes and lots of black hair. Bev provided lots of pretty pink accessories, including a frilly cover that she made herself for the bassinet. My sisters Gladys and Norma, who were living with us when Christine was born, doted on her. Gladys worked at an ugg boot shop in North Melbourne, and she brought a gorgeous pink pair home for the baby.

When Jim began to serenade us that night, Bev and I were desperately trying to go to sleep while hoping he wouldn't wake Christine. As it was, the boys had been woken, and my sisters couldn't sleep either.

At 3 a.m. Bev had had enough. 'Get a bucket of water and throw it over him.'

I didn't need much persuading—I threw the water down.

'Aaaaaaaahh!' Jim was shocked and drenched.

It worked a treat: all went quiet, and we finally got some sleep.

The bucket trick worked a couple of times, but the air-raid siren—as I called it—kept coming on again. Jim's night-piercing noise was just about loud enough to wake the dead.

Enter another idea. I got two thick woollen blankets from the linen cupboard, then went downstairs and convinced Jim to come for a ride with me. I told him I couldn't get to sleep so I might as well go for a drive—no trouble selling that. 'I haven't had a ride in your new Kombi van anyway,' he slurred.

I drove him as far as I could across the western suburbs and finished up in Sunshine. Then I saw the perfect location: a school. Every school still had a shelter shed in its grounds, and what else were the sheds for but to provide help during air-raids?

Just as well security was pretty relaxed in those days. I shone the torch around and found the shed without too much effort. When I'd put one of the blankets down on the long seat, I turned off the torch and sat in the darkness with Jim. He'd been clutching a bottle of wine all night and taking an occasional swig, getting drunker by the minute and dozing off periodically. I didn't have to suggest twice that he lie down and try to get some shut-eye. I sat at the other end of the bench and leant back with folded arms. Next moment I was woken up by the pungent smell of cheap wine on Jim's breath and his heavy snoring.

After covering him with the other blanket, I turned on my torch, walked swiftly out of the shed and drove home. It was nearly two in the morning.

My strategy worked like a charm. Jim certainly couldn't get back in time to air-raid any more that night and didn't make it in time for breakfast either. I was a little worried when he hadn't turned up for breakfast the next morning. The following morning, however, I was relieved to see him back and as large as life. Although there was no mention of the van ride, it was a long time before he air-raided us again!

~

After working with our men and occasional woman for a while, Bev and I became very protective of them, almost like they were our own children. They were an interesting line-up of people from all walks of life. One was the brother of a famous billiards player and a champion player in his own right. Another was a former chemist from a country town, and there was also an ex-priest forever wringing his hands. Alcohol is no respecter of rank.

In those days there was little tolerance by police for drunks. They would often get thrown unceremoniously into the back of a divvy van and then be tossed into a cell to sober up. Many told us of the police deliberately swerving the vehicle around so they would be thrown about, and speeding up and then braking suddenly so they would slide towards the front, sometimes getting hurt in the process. They would often then be taken before a magistrate and given a week or a fortnight in prison for being drunk and disorderly. Many alcoholics served considerable sentences on such an instalment plan. In all fairness, however, it probably saved their lives many times.

There was quite a high casualty rate for alcoholics in summer and winter. They would be so anaesthetised as they lay in the sun that they would get terribly sunburnt. Worse than that—oblivious to any blowflies around them, they would have maggots crawling over their open sores. Oddly, that was somewhat beneficial: maggots actually clean up wounds. In winter the alcoholics were oblivious to frostbite, and many had to have fingers and toes amputated. Any gaol sentences during summer or winter gave them respite from the elements. Bev and I scraped many maggots off flyblown people, and we took many of them, along with frostbitten people, to hospital.

The strict pub opening hours had contributed to the success of a very profitable black market in illegal alcohol, known as sly grog. Mixed businesses and grocery shops were often sly grog outlets; that was certainly so in North Melbourne, where men could readily obtain cheap wine in some of these stores at inflated prices. To me, that wasn't so bad—I understood that alcoholics had to obtain their booze by hook or crook. It was a mercenary matter of supply and demand.

What I strenuously objected to was the sale of methylated spirits to alcoholics. Metho is very toxic, and when imbibed it can cause severe nausea, blindness and even death. Working in casualty I had seen all the disastrous effects of methylated spirits.

It was illegal to sell metho to obvious alcoholics. Many of them told me where they bought it, so I was aware of businesses that sold it to them in North Melbourne. There was a main outlet that I had reported to the local police several times. One officer said he was handling the illegal alcohol report, but he told me that he could never catch the sly-grog place in the act and so couldn't get any evidence.

Incensed at the lack of progress, I decided to get the evidence for him. I didn't shower for a few days, then dressed in some of the mission men's smelly discarded clothes and scruffy shoes. I dabbed wine and methylated spirits on my clothing. Surprise surprise, I had no trouble obtaining metho at its very inflated price, and I did so on a number of occasions, feigning drunkenness each time.

I obtained quite a bit of evidence for the policeman, who then kept telling me all sorts of stories as to why the shop hadn't been raided and the culprits brought before the courts. Apparently the police station was short-staffed, or he had to be there in person for any raid, or he'd been away sick, or he had to attend to more important police business. The issue dragged on and on.

Then the alcoholics told me they couldn't buy metho at that place any longer, because some do-gooder was trying to get the shopkeeper charged. I realised he had been tipped off. The police-man was on the take, and it was my word against his. None of the alcoholics who knew he was corrupt would give evidence. It wasn't worth it—they would be cutting off their supply. He was never charged.

~

I went undercover on another occasion for a different reason. Time and time again, men at the mission gave me accounts of how badly they were treated by some of the religious institutions, notably some that provided accommodation. So once again I went unshaved and unkempt for a week, this time with my mate Jim, tramping around the streets of Melbourne during the day and sleeping in dosshouses at night.

It was an eye-opener: an unnerving, humiliating and enlightening experience. We were abused by pedestrians walking past us or by drivers stopped at lights. These people would call out such demeaning things as 'Get a job, bludgers!' 'Get off the streets! You're making them untidy.' 'You should all be locked up.' And much worse.

We would obtain breakfast discreetly at the side door of the mission, where we were handed sandwiches like others who didn't want to go inside and sit down. Bev would come out to check on me while being careful not to blow my cover. Then Jim and I would continue trudging around until lunchtime, when we would go to one of the religious places for a feed: the Hole in the Wall, run by the Sisters of Mercy in Carlton; the Gill Memorial Home for Men run by the Salvation Army in West Melbourne; or Ozanam House in North Melbourne, run by the St Vincent de Paul Society.

I was shocked by one of the religious dosshouses in particular, despite Jim and many others having told me about it. Seeing and experiencing it was to believe it. It was dirty and unkempt, and the beds that Jim and I slept in didn't look or smell like they had been changed in days. On the two nights we stayed there, the rostered staff spoke to us harshly and treated us like lesser mortals.

While there was no excuse for such treatment of vulnerable people, the work certainly wasn't easy. Brawls broke out periodically, and a firm hand was needed to contain them. Those in charge of religious dosshouses tended to be converts from a similar background to those in need of help. Perhaps this should have made the managers and staff more understanding and tolerant, but I assumed they had been recruited partly because they were streetwise and tough. Some of those I encountered appeared to be immature novices at the practice of patience and tolerance.

~

While Bev and I were happy with the philosophy of giving daily spiritual bread together with actual food each day, we believed there needed to be a specific targeted program for alcoholics at the centre. Ideally it would be a live-in program so that it could have a more continuous influence on attendees. We'd commenced Alcoholics Victorious or AV as a separate Saturday meeting, and quite a few men and some women were attending. So we decided to provide accommodation for up to ten men and feature AV as part of a Real Life Program that would include work- and incomed-oriented occupational therapy. The Real Life Program was designed by Bev and me to be a holistic, practical program that would incorporate all existing activities at the Centre plus any additional ones to ensure they catered for body and mind as well as spirit. I asked the mission maintenance man to fit out a ten-bed unit on the ground floor. The beds filled quickly, and what had mostly been morning work turned into fulltime work.

The attendees became part of our extended family, even eating an occasional meal with us. Jim, his brother Bill and another brother participated, and ultimately all three of them achieved sobriety. Jim took to the program like a duck to water, especially the Real Life Studies and occupational therapy.

We used lapidary work—the cutting and polishing of stones and gems—as occupational therapy, which enabled the men not only to have field trips to collect the materials but also to learn gem-making skills and earn some income. Bev's dad was very skilled at lapidary work and had trained me in it. We mainly used petrified wood that I obtained on trips to St George; the Balonne River was lined with the stuff, and I would gather up thousands of stones to bring back to the mission. We had a tumbling machine and a diamond-cutting blade. The finished stones were in all shapes and sizes, ideal for key rings as well as brooches, pendants and other jewellery items. Jim became quite proficient at lapidary work. He also became a great encourager and supporter, and an incredible example of perseverance and hope.

In 1971 the mission superintendent who had recruited me, the Reverend Ron Barnes, was replaced. The board of management and new superintendent put in place policies I didn't agree with. They believed there was no longer a place at the mission for spirituality, such as our devotional talks from the Bible over breakfast. I argued that the example of Jesus feeding the thousands physically while teaching them spiritually was a strong precedent for combining the spiritual with the practical, and that our new programs were an example of this. The mission wouldn't budge, so I had no option but to resign.

Bev was due to give birth to our fourth child in early June. During this turbulent period, we felt it would be best for her to go to her parents in St George for the birth and for some time afterwards. They were thrilled at the prospect, and it would give me time to sort out accommodation and pursue job prospects. She flew to Queensland in mid-May. All the children went with Bev. A great opportunity for them to bond with their relatives in Queensland.

Just before we left the Melbourne City Mission, the superintendent of the Brisbane City Mission offered me the superintendency there. I declined. Bev and I believed that it wasn't meant to be, despite the mission being in her home state.

I had arranged a speaking tour through Victoria, New South Wales and Queensland during May with a group of former alcoholics from the mission. We decided to schedule our meetings so that we would arrive in St George by 3 June, Bev's due date. I would keep in touch with her along the way in case there were indications the birth was going to happen earlier. The third of June was my father-in-law's birthday, and he was hoping against hope that our baby would be born then.

A funny and frustrating incident took place when we were coming through New South Wales. I'd purchased a brand new mini-bus prior to the trip. A Daihatsu twelve-seater with a solid roof rack. Just outside Newcastle, it broke down. The battery light had been on for a long time, indicating that the battery hadn't been charging, and more than likely the alternator had stopped working.

I left the men in the bus and hitchhiked to the vehicle dealership in Newcastle to get a replacement alternator and see if that would rectify the problem. Fortunately the dealer had a spare, and he offered to drive me back to the bus and fit it for me. The only problem was that when we got to the place where I had left the bus, it wasn't there!

'Are you sure this is where you left it?' the dealer asked.

'Absolutely! I clearly remember driving to this point. If I was a betting man I would bet anything that I'm right.'

We drove up and down until it was nearly dark. Still no bus.

'If you're certain this is where you left it, you need to get the police involved. I'll drive you to the station if you like.'

So he did, and I was soon in a highway patrol car repeating the procedure. Except that this time the questioning was more intense.

'Could those you left behind get the bus going?' the police officer asked.

'No.'

'Could any of them drive it?'

'Probably.'

'Are they trustworthy?'

'Yes.'

'By the way, when you got onto the freeway, did you pay a toll?'

'No.'

'You must have been on the old freeway, not the tollway! I'll take you.'

The bus and the men were there! It was dark by then, but the patrolman was very gracious about it, using the spotlight on his car so I could fit the alternator. It did the job.

The men had been pretty frustrated and worried, but they were quite understanding and amused when they heard the story. They ribbed me for a long time afterwards, saying, 'How could you lose a whole bus and its passengers?'

They were very subdued, however, while the policeman was there—conscious that most of them had records, and one or two of them probably had outstanding warrants.

~

The timing of my arrival in St George was pretty close to the wind. Our last speaking engagement had been in Dalby the night before, just over three hundred kilometres away. It was an important meeting arranged by my old mentors Jack and Ollie Evans, who were keen to hear from the men attending Alcoholics Victorious and the Real Life Program. The meeting was held in the Presbyterian church that the Evanses attended, and a lot of people were present, from other churches as well. The former alcoholics spoke of becoming Christians and achieving sobriety. After they finished telling their stories, I invited anyone present needing to gain sobriety to commit themselves to this task. Seven men and a woman responded, which was encouraging.

We arrived at St George in the nick of time, late in the afternoon the following day. Bev had been in mild labour for some hours. We all went to bed pretty tired, especially Bev, who was having labour pains. These intensified at about 10 p.m., and I took her to hospital. Pamela Joy was born three hours later, an incredible joy to me and Bev, and the only one of our children to be born in Queensland. She came into the world with a smile on her face and was nicknamed 'Smiley'.

Bev's dad should have been called 'Smiley' at that time also. Although Pamela was born an hour after his birthday, he thought this didn't count. He just about had a perpetual smile on his face and kept doing his famous Fred Astaire two-step dance of happiness.

I stayed in St George for a few days to visit my wife and baby in hospital, and to be with them when they got out. It was an enormous blessing to have two sons and two daughters, for Bev to have had a normal birth again, for mother and daughter to be very well, and for Bev to be able to spend this special time with her family. She and Pamela stayed with her parents for a few weeks. Meanwhile, the men and I drove leisurely back to Melbourne and took time out for some sightseeing. Most of them hadn't been interstate before.

14

New horizons

After leaving the Melbourne City Mission, Bev and I and co-workers and support from the original Mission endeavoured to establish what we called the Melbourne Rescue Mission. There was a very keen committee, and a lot of written and vocal support, but not enough financial support.

In Bev's absence I put a deposit on an old weatherboard house in the western suburb of Sunshine. It had a large bungalow to accommodate our guests and was very well priced. However, I was so anxious to make provision for Bev, our young family and the men that I didn't check the house thoroughly. That it didn't have hot water in the kitchen didn't faze me—I would get hot water put on. But there were no certified building inspections before house sales in those days, and I soon discovered that there was a fine line between faith and foolishness.

Arriving home with a newborn, Bev was horrified by the state of the place. She went over it with a fine-tooth comb and found, of all things, borers throughout the house. Having only one eye was no excuse for having missed them! There was no way we could go ahead with the purchase, and we lost our deposit.

We rented a five-bedroom brick home on a quiet street in the north-east suburb of Ascot Vale. It only had a small backyard but was very comfortable. Three of the men from the Real Life Program shifted in with us, despite our now having four young children. The men were happy knowing they were part of our extended family, as they had been in North Melbourne, eating meals and going on outings with us.

I worked two jobs for about nine months to keep bread and butter on the table. I was a full-time cleaner at an auto-parts business by day, and a part-time door-to-door salesman with a wedding trousseaux company in the evening. I received the National Salesman of the Month Award on one occasion. Bev did incredibly hard yards, as you can imagine, with four young kids and three men in the house while I was out working a lot of the time.

Out of the blue in mid-1972, I was contacted by the Reverend Ron Barnes, the former superintendent of the Melbourne City Mission, who had become a church minister in Ballarat. The Ballarat Town and City Mission was seeking a new superintendent and a mission sister, and he had recommended me and Bev for the roles. After praying about it, we were sure we should go to Ballarat for an interview.

～

Although Bev and I had visited Ballarat previously, it was like a breath of fresh air for us. Literally fresh because of its very cool climate! It was nostalgic for both of us as well. For Bev because it was very similar to Toowoomba, with a similar population of around sixty thousand, and for both of us as a city with a very friendly and welcoming country town atmosphere. I appreciated its history, as the city of the Eureka Stockade and the Eureka Rebellion, believed to have given birth to Australia's democracy, and its many wonderful early-nineteenth-century buildings and statues. Ballarat is the city of statues. I must say I did say to Bev, 'We'll never be statues, we'll always be active here!'

The Ballarat City Mission was more like a church than a drop-in centre. It had two church services every Sunday, as well as Sunday school, a youth club, netball teams, and an opportunity shop. It offered extensive welfare assistance, including food and clothing, through the op shop. Its facilities were a mixture of the old and new. It had a large old activities hall plus tennis and netball courts. It also had a new chapel, opportunity shop complex, toilets and offices. It looked out over the large Mission Reserve opposite with spacious picnic areas and an amazing old Chinese joss house still intact with a high front step to trip up evil spirits trying to get in. When I asked the Board what went on in the Mission hall, they said one of its main uses was as a boxing gym. In fact the guy who ran it was Bobby Greville. I knew of Bobby as the noted Victorian boxing champion. He had defeated Andre Famechon, Johnny Famechon's father, in the Victorian welterweight boxing title, my division.

The Golden Point Football Club in the Ballarat Football League had originally been the mission's football team. In the early nineteenth-century goldrush era, a Chinese church had been attached to the mission. Older residents told of the sight of Chinese people in traditional colourful dress and hairstyles with pigtails as they walked in single file to church. The Chinese residents were sadly much despised and maligned because the white residents thought they were taking too much gold and sending it back to their country. But the mission embraced, supported and advocated strongly for them; the staff also taught them Aussie Rules football and integrated them into the mission team. The Golden Point Football Club jumpers had 'Rice Eaters' proudly emblazoned on the back.

The mission board of management evidently liked what they saw in me and Bev, and we liked what we saw of the mission work and its prospects. We didn't hesitate to accept the offer of appointment as mission superintendent and mission sister. At twenty-nine years of age I was the youngest superintendent in their 105-year history, and Bev the youngest mission sister by far at twenty-five years old.

Bev's role would be to coordinate the women's and children's work, including the Sunday school and management of the op shop with its associated welfare work. My role would be to oversee the mission's activities as a whole, to be its visionary and driver, and to be its community and governmental spokesman. I would also be its pastor, taking two services each Sunday and being responsible for its general pastoral care.

We had it all ahead of us—how exciting! The only drawback was that the incumbent superintendent and mission sister weren't retiring until the end of the year, so we would not start work until January 1973 but could shift into the mission manse over Christmas.

After making sure our three house guests had alternative accommodation, we duly moved into the manse at the end of December 1972. The mission was a respected institution, and our neighbours were very welcoming, some calling in to say hello and give us home-cooked goodies.

~

Jim Bentley and Chuck Mendenhall had shifted to Ballarat to assist us in the work, and we were very happy about that. Chuck had been working for the Ford Motor Company in Melbourne, so he transferred to a Ford motor reconditioning plant in Ballarat. Jim moved in with us, and Chuck found his own lodgings.

Jim had enjoyed a fairly long period of sobriety. He seemed to be thriving as part of the mission team and of our extended family. He was back in contact with some of his own family and was loving it. Then one night he didn't come home. We waited up quite late for him but he didn't show up. Being new to Ballarat, we had no idea where he might be. Like we would have for our own child under these circumstances, and especially for Jim as an alcoholic who had the propensity to get into a lot of trouble, we feared the worst.

Then early the following morning, the air-raid siren that we had almost forgotten about sounded outside our window. Jim had broken out on the booze again. But I had my tried and true method to stop the siren.

I didn't know the area but drove Jim about ten kilometres away and dropped him in the tiny township of Buninyong. It was a warm summer night, so I drove home satisfied that he'd be all right, and that Bev and the kids would be able to get some more sleep.

I made a slight detour to the top of Mount Buninyong to view the Ballarat city lights I'd heard so much about, then drove home slowly, savouring the triumph.

When I arrived at our gateway, there to my shock and horror was Jim. Someone who had recognised him from the mission church, and knew he was living with us, had brought him home!

Remarkably he had sobered up considerably. I took him out to the bungalow at the back of our house, then sat down and had a frank chat with him. I told him how much Bev and the children, especially the baby, needed some sleep after having been woken up by him earlier. 'Sorry, mate,' he said with a slight slur, 'I could do with some sleep myself.' A few moments later he was out like a light.

~

When Bev and I started at the Mission and I had finally met Bobby Greville, he really touched a chord in me. As a Christian, Bobby had a heart for underprivileged teenagers and was teaching them to box while engaging with them and mentoring them, through sport! Coming across Bobby and sport in this way really challenged my thinking about sport and its place in religion. Prior to my conversion, sport had probably been my god; I had loved it and been totally committed to it. But although sport was my saviour from time to time, it never fully satisfied me. I would become very attracted to a sport and pursue it passionately, only to have the satisfaction dissipate. I then found there was no comparison to the permanent satisfaction Jesus had given me. Back then I had read a verse from the Bible that seemed to say I should put sport behind me: 'If anyone is into Christ he is a new person, old things have passed away and all things have become new.' I wrongly took that to mean that sport had passed away and that there was no longer any place for it in my Christian life. Seeing the work Bobby was doing among underprivileged youth was a defining moment for me as far as sport and spirituality were concerned.

It was 1973 and I hadn't participated in sport since October 1964, some months after I had become a Christian. Now I was convinced that not only was there a place for sport again in my life but that it could be used as a spiritual drawcard as well.

Enter Tony Raffety, a trailblazer for the toughest endurance sport in the world: ultramarathon running! Tony was the first to run from Melbourne to Sydney, and Sydney to Melbourne return. He then ran through Death Valley in California—the hottest place on earth—a feat previously thought impossible. He held the 1000-mile or 1609-kilometre world record for seven years. The great publicity he received caused a real resurgence of ultramarathons.

Tony inspired and challenged me to take up endurance running and use it to put Christianity on the map—and demonstrate that Christians were anything but weak and non-enduring. Early in our first year at the Ballarat mission, I started training for a 230-kilometre run to Melbourne and back. I would be raising funds for the mission's Winter Appeal—to buy blankets and food, and to assist with emergency accommodation—and hopefully be helping to put Christianity on the map. Six days a week I was on the road by 4 a.m., hail, rain or shine; I would run thirty kilometres before breakfast, and then take a longer run, usually about fifty kilometres, each Saturday.

July 1973 found me on the road commencing my first ultra-marathon. An ultramarathon run is any distance further than the marathon distance of 42.195 kilometres. Chuck Mendenhall was my handler, and Jim and Eddie were vehicle drivers and part of my support crew. Eddie did a lot of running with me as well. Eddie and I had always been pretty close, and were never really apart for long. Despite leading separate, busy lives, we would catch up with each other and support one another whenever we could.

My run had been advertised as a nonstop journey, but it wasn't literally that. By Guinness World Record rules, while running an ultramarathon you were allowed to have toilet breaks, massages and medical treatments. I ran to Melbourne and back to Footscray without a stop other than for ablutions. At Footscray I called in at an old friend's house for a quick shower, and was on the road again pretty quickly.

By about 2 a.m. I was running up the quite steep and drawn-out Pentland Hills past Bacchus Marsh. I was totally exhausted—in fact, I was worse than that. I was severely dehydrated and hallucinating. Animals were appearing on the road in front of me: giant kangaroos and wombats, and enormous koalas. Chuck was riding alongside me on a bike, urging me on, wondering why I was jumping sideways sometimes or running behind the bike as a shield. I kept saying, 'The wind,' but there wasn't much wind. I didn't let on that I was hallucinating.

I had no idea about dietary requirements for such a mammoth physical undertaking. I was simply eating the food I would normally consume during my working week—food such as lamb and pickle sandwiches, or egg, tomato and cheese sandwiches, or even steak sandwiches—which didn't easily get digested and floated around in my stomach like lead weights, and nauseated me. My liquid intake was orange juice only, which became quite caustic in my stomach. Then I stopped eating altogether. No wonder I felt so depleted.

Early that morning Bev had a premonition that something wasn't right with me. Eddie's wife Rhonda was staying with her, and they drove down the road to find me out on my feet, oblivious to everyone and everything around me, just running by muscle memory, one foot after the other.

Bev took one look at me and said to Chuck, 'Stop. He's got to stop. He will die if he doesn't stop!' Melodramatic stuff, but possibly true.

'He can't stop,' said Chuck. 'This is supposed to be a nonstop run.'

'I don't care what it's supposed to be,' replied Bev. 'He needs an hour or two of sleep, and then he'll make much better time than he's able to do now anyway.'

Eddie stopped the support bus. Thus commenced a battle for my body, with toing and froing between Bev and Chuck as to why I should or shouldn't stop running. Bev won the battle. I stopped, had a good sleep and ran on considerably refreshed. Chuck, meanwhile, had got into a huff about my stopping and resting, and he rode off on his bike in the dark, not to be seen again for a good long while.

About twenty kilometres from Ballarat, I hit the wall again. Eddie was running with me and encouraging me, but he was very tired also—he had run a long way and done a lot of slow, tiring driving behind me. I was praying like crazy to be able to finish the run. Then two amazing things happened: a busload of young people from our youth club turned up with Bobby Greville and ran with me, and then it started to rain lightly!

I had run from the Ballarat Town Hall to Melbourne Town Hall and back to the town of Ballan, and I had a deadline to run onto the North Ballarat Football Ground at half-time during the footy match. I had to keep going.

'You can do it, Bill! *Go!*' they kept saying, and together with the refreshing rain, their encouragement gave me a new spring in my step. I was high-stepping it and bantering like I had just started the run, forgetting that I was exhausted. With the light rain continuing to fall, it felt like I was constantly running through an invigorating shower.

I arrived right on schedule to do a lap of honour at half-time. What a testament to the power of encouragement! The run was front-page news, and our mission and my running became increasingly newsworthy from that point on.

~

Our work at the Ballarat City Mission was vastly different to our work at the Melbourne City Mission. We still worked with many vulnerable people, but our roles were family oriented, so we had programs for children, teenagers and adults. I was quite entrepreneurial in attracting young people to our programs. Purchasing a Shetland pony and naming him Sunday School was one way of doing this. I taught him to nod his head and indicate 'yes' and 'no' and lie down and play dead. The young people at the Mission thought it was hilarious when I asked Sunday School if I was the best-looking, smartest, and most muscular person there, and he gave an up and down affirmative nod!

One of the first new programs we started was for children in primary and secondary school, and it was attended by many kids from the schools where Bev and I gave religious instruction. We wanted to reach out to marginalised young people, and train and mentor them for positive prospects in their futures, so we commenced an Awana Club. (Awana stands for Approved Workers Are Not Ashamed, and while it was Biblically orientated, it was also very holistic and encouraged young people to do their best at everything.)

We had over a hundred young people in the club. Some parents would drop off and pick up their children, and the rest we bussed in from across Ballarat. Ellis, who was now my spiritual brother, travelled four hundred kilometres every weekend to assist with the program. The club was professionally operated, requiring every leader to do a thorough leadership course before being allowed to participate. Just as importantly, leaders were selected on the basis of their belief in the positive future for young people, their affable and winsome personalities, and their zest for life, qualities that would have a good influence.

The kids were very competitive and took to Awana keenly, and the club became the highlight of their week. It was sports focused, with specific team games played at the weekly meetings. In addition, each kid obtained higher ranks in the club the more they achieved at study. The club was uniformed, which brought about a visual equality: most of our young people were from lower socioeconomic backgrounds, and although some were from quite affluent families, in Awana they were one.

The culmination of each club year was the Awana State Games in Melbourne. Our young people were excited and nervous when the first big day arrived, but some of the glances towards our bus load of mission kids indicated there were doubts as to how they would behave or perform. Everyone soon found out that our young people were immaculately dressed and impeccably behaved. They scooped the pool of awards and received the championship trophy! When we took a team photograph after triumphantly arriving home, our kids nearly burst out of their uniforms with justifiable pride.

Chuck came into his own in the practical Mission work in Ballarat. He collected and delivered donated bread, fruit, vegetables and wood to needy people, as well as groceries from our own stores. We arranged for food to be delivered by rail from the Victorian Government Relief Centre in Melbourne, which Chuck picked up as well. He also transported many young people to and from a number of Mission activities. He was also one of the uniformed leaders in Awana, and as a former marine, that suited him well.

Ellis and Jim were also incredible associates in their own way. Ellis still worked and lived in Wycheproof and made the four-hundred-kilometre round trip to assist in the Awana program every Friday night, staying over the weekend to help in any way he could. Jim saw Bev and me and our children as part of his extended family, and we saw him the same way. Our children always addressed him as Uncle Jim. He had come such a long way. He had achieved sobriety and purchased his own home, and here he was now as a uniformed Awana leader and assisting Chuck on his pick-up and delivery rounds whenever he could. It was wonderful, three ex-soldiers, Chuck, Ellis and Jim, uniformed again, this time to assist needy young people. They were nicknamed 'the three amigos'.

The year 1975 was a momentous time in Chuck's life. Margaret Patti had been a student at MBI before Chuck and I. She then worked at the Coles Cafeteria in central Melbourne, where I got to know her through collecting leftover food for the Men's Centre. She visited Bev and I in Ballarat, where we introduced her to Chuck. Upon meeting each other they both felt an immediate attraction. I officiated at their wedding in December. They had a home of their own not far from the Mission and Margaret helped the Mission and its programs whenever she could. She often hosted some of our children at her house after school.

~

In the 1970s in Ballarat, all netball was played in a church competition. It was 1976, and the mission had a junior and a senior netball team. They hadn't played in finals in living memory. My family and I went along to watch the mission team play every week, rain, hail or shine. I couldn't stand to see our girls getting beaten substantially week after week, so I decided to coach our senior team.

There were no other male coaches, to my knowledge, in the netball competition at that time, so it remained to be seen how I would go. I was well into my ultramarathon-running career by now, and at the peak of fitness—hence, fitness and endurance were at the top of my training agenda for the girls. Their skill levels were quite high, as were their confidence and self-esteem, but they lacked consistency and endurance.

One of the best players in the Ballarat netball competition at that time was Robyn Gull. She played for the stand-out team, and she was a stand-out player—and our nemesis. My girls were quite intimidated and inhibited by her, so I sowed and watered the seeds that had been instilled in me 'You are anyone's equal'. But they found this hard to believe.

I decided to boost their confidence and self-esteem by making them super fit—I would take them out on the road for long hard runs. But this strategy almost ended on the first run. They mutinied, refusing to go any further. 'This is madness! We're not marathon runners, we're netball players.'

All protested, except one: Carol Seiler, our tall, solid, affable goal shooter. She said it all for me. 'You're right, we're not marathon runners, but we are barely netball players either. We are easybeats! I'm sure we're the laughing-stock of many other teams, and I hate it. What have we got to lose by giving Bill's coaching tactics a go for this season?'

They reluctantly followed her lead. Surprise, surprise, they became very competitive and weren't eliminated until the preliminary final.

Nineteen seventy-six had been a big year. Our netball girls had performed incredibly well, and Bev and I had received some wonderful news: she was expecting our fifth child, due date June 1977. After we'd had our first four children in five years, there had been almost a six-year break. Our kids were very excited—the boys wanted another brother, and the girls another sister.

Come the 1977 netball season, and our team were eager to resume training. You have never seen such a transformation—their confidence and self-esteem and endurance were sky-high. They had come to believe that given the right training, the right fitness, and the right skill levels, they were any team's equal. There was no more lowering of eyes when they encountered Robyn Gull or any other top player on the courts. By the middle of the season, the girls were undefeated, and I was thrilled with their progress.

Then an event occurred that skyrocketed everyone's spirits further. On Tuesday, 21 June 1977 at 1 p.m., an angel appeared in the form of our fifth child, Angela Maree. She was born with auburn hair, blue eyes and the fairest skin, and our other children thought she was a real-life angel.

Our netball team were very excited about Angela's birth also. Two days later, at our next training session, the team captain called the girls into a huddle and said to them quite passionately, 'We're gunna win Saturday's match for Bill and Bev, and for Angela. Angela! Angela! Angela!'

And win they did, beating the opposition by an even bigger margin than they had the year before. There was further great jubilation when the mission girls won the 1977 Netball Grand Final. The solid training had paid off.

Carol Seiler became a highly qualified and well-respected nurse in the Ballarat community. Robyn Gull had an amazing basketball career: a bronze medallist in the Atlanta Olympic Games, she was inducted into the Australian Basketball Hall of Fame.

~

The great thing about our mission work thus far was that not only had there never been a dull moment, but as if to compensate for disappointments from time to time, there were many rewarding experiences as well—even in the form of sad experiences. Such was the case when the phone rang in my office one day. I could barely hear the very quiet, husky voice at the other end. 'Pastor Bill?'

'Yes.'

'Can you come around, please?' There was a shrill urgency in the voice.

His address was only about ten minutes away, and I was able to go straight there. The house had seen better days. It was an old miner's cottage that had been added onto a number of times. The gardens were overrun, lawns unmown. Blinds were drawn at the front of the house, and cobwebs were over the front door.

I didn't bother knocking there and went around to a side door. *Rap-rap-rap.* No answer. I did it a number of times before I could hear some faint sounds: a voice and a shuffling noise. The shuffling was getting closer. 'It's Pastor Bill!' I shouted, probably louder than I needed to.

I heard an indecipherable response. There was a lot more shuffling and scratching at the door, which finally edged open. The sight that confronted me made me think of Jim's accounts of the prisoner-of-war camps: a snowy-haired man in an absolutely emaciated condition, just skin and bone and sunken eyes. His legs were bowed, and he was only being held up by the door as he clutched it. 'Thank you,' he whispered. I had to grab him and hold him before he fell. 'Can you help me to my bedroom?' he rasped.

I carried him there. The smell in the house was so overwhelming that I felt like dry-retching. And the gentleman in my arms was part of it—unwashed, unkempt, unchanged.

I sat him on the edge of his bed, which was something else, filthy and putrid. The obvious human emergency overrode it all, however. The dear old man couldn't sit up, but he didn't want to lie down either. 'I need to take you to hospital. Can I get you a drink?'

'No, not yet. Thank you for coming. I want you to do something for me before I die.'

'Sure.'

He pointed to a soiled, dog-eared old hymnbook lying on his bed. 'It was my wife's. She loved it and always used to sing from it. I hated it. Gave her such a hard time. I'm so sorry now. I miss her so much. I love these songs now. I just want to go to her. Will you sing with me, Pastor Bill?'

'Of course I will. Just call me Bill, though.'

We sang away, tears streaming down our faces. 'What a Friend We Have in Jesus', then 'When the Roll Is Called up Yonder', followed by 'There Is Sunshine in My Soul Today'. I held the hymnbook in one hand and the precious old man against me with the other, so that he wouldn't fall over.

I don't want to exaggerate this, but I'm sure that despite my friend's enormous frailty and the fragility of his vocal cords, a miracle occurred. His voice recovered. I wouldn't say he became a leading tenor, but all of a sudden I realised that he was belting out these great old hymns with me. A young man and an old man, we were singing our hearts out through the book.

I have no idea how long I was there. Time stood still. The title of one of the hymns was, 'Heaven Came Down and Glory Filled My Soul', and that's what had happened.

The dear old man then told me an incredibly upsetting story. His wife had belonged to a particular denomination. Prior to contacting me, he had reached out to the minister of her church. This man had gone around to the side door as I had. When the door was opened, however: 'He gave a look of revulsion, turned up his nose

186

and offered every excuse as to why he couldn't stay, then walked away, not to come back.'

Because of the prominence I'd gained through my ultramarathon running and work at the mission, I was newsworthy, and my inspirational messages were regularly printed in the *Ballarat Courier*. The old man's wife used to read them and share them with him, and so he had contacted me.

I called an ambulance and got him to hospital. He died not long after. He didn't want to live here any longer; he just wanted to join his wife in Heaven.

Bev has a favourite saying, 'People matter more than things.' I believe that my contact with this man in many ways represented our work in Ballarat and elsewhere. Whoever people were and whatever their circumstances, we were driven to give them whatever help they needed.

15

Revival

The end of 1977, a momentous year for me and Bev, found us reflecting on the past decade. I was twenty-four when we got married, and Bev twenty; we were now only thirty-four and thirty, yet we had five beautiful children and had achieved major mission leadership roles in Melbourne and Ballarat. I had travelled across Australia speaking at mission conferences and was making a mark as an ultramarathon runner. All this despite our circumstances and qualifications. Around this time I had an unusual experience. A woman knocked at our front door and said she had a message from God for me. I let her in with great interest. She'd discovered that I had an artificial eye and said God had told her that if I had enough faith, He would replace it with a normal eye. I hadn't considered such a proposition before, and I must say that when I observed the messenger wearing glasses, I did think it was the pot calling the kettle black! Her words really made me think, however, and after she had gone I found myself reminiscing about what my life had been like with an artificial eye. I came to the conclusion that the eye had been a great asset, and I wouldn't want to be without it.

Some funny memories flooded back to me. I thought of how my children had firmly believed, until they were three or four years old, that when I took out my eye it could actually see. Sometimes when I was looking after them while Bev was out, I would remove my eye, put it on the table and say, 'You'd better behave yourselves—I'll be keeping an eye on you!' They were *very* well behaved indeed!

I was also reminded of how being a one-eyed prison visitor had softened many of the hardest prisoners, beginning with those I'd met while doing work experience at Pentridge, and continuing with guys I'd met in Melbourne and Ballarat who were now in gaol.

Although I wasn't a smoker or a gambler, I would say to a prisoner who didn't know I had an artificial eye, 'I bet you a couple of packets I can chew on my eye.'

You could just about see them thinking, *I've seen blokes with tongues long enough to lick their eyebrows, but I don't know about being able to chew on their eye . . .*

'Yes, I can,' I'd insist.

'Oh, all right,' they'd inevitably respond, obviously only to pacify me.

Then I would take out my eye, put it in my mouth and chew on it!

They'd be amazed. Their reactions ranged from shock to nausea, but always involved great amusement.

Then, to really confuse them, I would say, 'Look, I was a bit of a mongrel conning you like that. Tell you what, double or nothing I can chew on my other eye.'

Their minds would really have been racing, probably thinking I was feeling sorry for them and giving them a chance to win.

'Okay then,' they would say—and out would come my dentures, and I'd use them to chew on my eye!

~

During the 1960s and 1970s there was a strong emphasis on revival and faith healing in many churches around the world. While I believed that God could do anything I was sceptical of many of the accounts of healing. Some reports seemed exaggerated, and many were without medical evidence that the ailment had existed in the first place.

The German theologian and writer Kurt E. Koch had a keen interest in this area, and his book *Revival in Indonesia* had been published in 1970. I was impressed with his balanced and honest writing, and I corresponded with him during 1979. Kurt told me about the revival among the Zulus; he said it had been occurring since 1966, and that thousands of Zulus had become Christians in that time. He believed that many of them had been helped or healed through faith and that drug addicts and alcoholics had been cured. He wrote, something like 'With many things in life there is the real and there is the counterfeit. That is especially true in the spiritual realm, and with accounts of revival, but I am convinced that the real thing is occurring in South Africa amongst the Zulus at the moment. The best thing to do always is to check things out at first hand if at all possible. Why don't you go to South Africa and see and decide for yourself what is happening?'

This was the challenge of challenges. After much prayer and consultation with Bev, I was convinced I should go. Chuck Mendenhall wanted to go with me, and we flew out to South Africa on 26 January 1980.

I had flown domestically a number of times to attend conferences, but this was my first international flight. I found myself reflecting that the only flying on my radar prior to the change in my life was when I'd dreamt myself as a sparrowhawk! Australian kids who were low on the socioeconomic scale, as I had been, didn't have thoughts of flying internationally. I was fortunate that throughout my life, my mentors had encouraged me to reach for the stars. Now this felt literal.

Arriving at Johannesburg airport was unnerving. Heavily armed soldiers were everywhere. The summer temperature outside was a pleasant twenty-six degrees on a sunny day. The city itself was of great contrast: it had many modern buildings and affluent areas and a lot of slum areas as well. The country around was full of contrasts also; to the north and west of the city were undulating hills while the eastern parts were flatter and well grassed.

We were to travel to a revivalist mission in the town of Mapumulo, south of the city of Pietermaritzburg. This was during the dark days of apartheid. We travelled by train and bus, and when we were in areas governed by whites it was appalling to see segregated toilets on the train platforms. The carriages were segregated also: those for whites would sometimes be half full, while those for blacks would be overcrowded.

After staying at the Kwa Sizabantu Mission for four weeks, and interviewing many of those who claimed to have been helped or healed through faith, we felt convinced that something special and good had indeed happened and was still happening.

While staying at the mission we met a couple of white revivalists who maintained they had been healed—but not physically. They said that the eyes of their minds had been opened to recognise that we are all God's creations, and in His sight all are precious and all are equal. At Kwa Sizabantu, people from all backgrounds were seeking and observing and working together in harmony. Apartheid simply didn't exist there. It was amazing to experience.

I met a former alcoholic who had bashed his wife countless times. She had gone to Kwa Sizabantu, become a Christian there, and experienced great peace and hope—so much so that her husband recognised something special had happened in her life. He said he would like to go there and get help also, providing he could take a supply of alcohol with him. She doubted that was possible but checked with one of the leaders, who said, 'He needs help. Let him come as he is and bring what he wants. God will sort it out.' So the husband put a carton of beer on the back seat of his car and drove to Kwa Sizabantu. On the long driveway into the mission, he hit a bump—and every bottle of beer broke. He said out loud, 'God is in this place', and became a committed Christian. It was some years after this incident that I spoke to him and his wife, a very happy couple who were adamant they had received a lasting resource for their lives and marriage.

~

When I arrived back in Australia in late February 1980, a number of things stood out for me about my experience of revival at Kwa Sizabantu. That God really is a miracle-working God. That a deep, sweeping revival of Christianity can occur anywhere. That it is what some countries desperately need. That a genuine revival is a balanced revival that heals the heart and mind primarily, and sometimes the body. However, what most people consider revival is perhaps not revival itself but the result of revival. Biblical revival is firstly about individual Christians returning to grass roots, to a close relationship with Jesus. Simply and earnestly following Jesus and his examples and teaching, particularly his admonition to 'Love the Lord your God with all your heart and with all your soul and with all your mind, and your neighbour as yourself.' Because love never fails—it overflows to touch relatives and friends and neighbours and some-times whole countries.

I found it very hard to settle down to normal living after having experienced revival and communal living. To begin with, I was fired up to share what I had witnessed, and many churches were eager to hear my accounts. I not only convened meetings at the mission and elsewhere for that purpose, but others did in their churches also.

In the middle of all this, in early June 1980, Bev and I were given the wonderful news that she was expecting our sixth child in March the following year. Our kids were really excited again. Our eldest, David, was now twelve, and our youngest, Angela, was almost four. She was old enough to be not just excited about a baby coming but also at thoughts of a baby girl—wow! Her older sisters, nine and ten years old, were well and truly old enough to be brainwashing her into chanting, 'Baby girl! Baby girl! Baby girl!'

Throughout the year there was no escaping the effect that Kwa Sizabantu had on me. I was especially enthralled by the concept of co-workers living communally while reaching out to people in need. I prayed about it, and I talked about it incessantly with colleagues. Chuck, Bev and Jim were sold on the idea, as were another couple, John and Jeanette Lowe, who were members of our mission congregation and strong supporters.

In order to achieve our goals, we'd need to take some very bold steps. To start with, we would need to purchase a reasonably large block of land and build a suitable facility. But for me, the boldest step of all would be to resign my position as superintendent of the Ballarat City Mission and live without an assured income. Before this major decision, I fasted and prayed extensively, spending seven days alone in the bush near Ballarat to get clarity of mind and direction.

On the seventh day, I had a vision. It was of a very narrow, heavily timbered block of land at the foot of a mountain. There was a steep slope on the northern side running south, and a steep slope on the southern side running north. Between the slopes there was a gully with a creek. Some words came to mind: 'You shall live in a low, low place where the hail comes down in the forest.'

Back home, I shared this vision with Bev and my associates. They were as assured as I was that there may well be something in it. In fact, I was so convinced that I drove around looking for the property I had seen.

Having been impressed with the mudbrick villages or kraals in South Africa, I was interested in building with this material. There was an architect who specialised in mudbrick construction near

Ballarat, so I paid him a visit. He asked me where I was going to build, and I told him about my vision, half expecting he would think I was a religious nut.

What followed sent a shiver up my spine. 'The block you've described to me, Bill, is just down the road. It's for sale.'

There could not have been a more excited man who drove the twelve kilometres out to look at this block—and what I saw blew me away. It was narrow but very long, nearly nine hectares, just below Mount Buninyong on the western side. Very heavily timbered, the block sloped down to a gully on the northern and southern sides.

I immediately went home and rang the agent's number on the For Sale sign. He told me the property had been sold, that somebody had only just signed for it. Unbelievable! But for some reason, I felt a strange peace about this.

The next day I drove out to the block with Chuck, who was just as excited about it as I was. While we were there, a dairy farmer who lived next door came over. He knew me through the publicity about my running and about the Ballarat City Mission. 'Interested in buying it, Bill?'

'I was, but the real estate agent tells me it's sold.'

In passing the farmer told me who owned the property: a doctor who just happened to be my sister's GP.

It was the Queen's Birthday long weekend 1980, a Saturday. On Monday morning I was up at about five for my devotions, as my custom was, and it came to my mind: *Ring the doctor.* I argued against the thought: *It's a long weekend. He will think I'm mad.* But finally the voice got so loud and so persistent that I could no longer resist.

I waited until after 9 a.m., located his house number and rang. To my surprise, he answered his phone. I was all apologetic. My opening words were, 'You'll think I'm crazy, but . . .' I went on to tell him the whole story.

The good doctor said something that still astounds me. 'It doesn't matter, Bill. You can have the property. Fulfil your vision.'

I was speechless. Then I said, 'Are you sure it's all right? You've already signed for it.'

'Bill, it's my property. I'm telling you, you can have it. Not as a gift, of course, but for $9500.'

It might as well have been a gift.

The final test as to whether it was meant to be was a consultation with my wife and associates. They were just as convinced as I was. I rang the doctor back and said we would take it.

~

We named our property Genesis Christian Mission. Genesis is the first book of the Old Testament, and it means 'in the beginning', the first words in the Bible. We wanted our property to be a place of new beginnings for many needy people.

We needed to give the mission plenty of time to replace me and Bev, so we made our resignations to be effective from January 1981, just a couple of months before Bev's due date. I stopped ultramarathon running for a while to concentrate on developing our block.

Settlement wasn't until August 1980, and as soon as we got access to the property we were out there every spare moment—after school and on our days off, as well as Saturdays. We extensively cleared a couple of hectares at the front of the the block in preparation for the temporary facilities and a concrete slab to go down for our house. The children had a ball exploring the property and climbing its trees, and helping to make mudbricks. There were a lot of cries of 'Yuck!' as they squished their feet in the moulds.

Prior to our move onto Genesis, I went to the Buninyong Council and told them that we wanted to build our own home but that it would be a while before we could. I asked what we could do in the interim. 'Don't broadcast this,' they told me, 'but we have a by-law that states that if you leave the wheels on a caravan, you can attach anything you like to it, and it's classified as an annexe.' We purchased a number of caravans, then made thousands of mudbricks and built rooms for our older children, connecting them as annexes to the caravans—while leaving the wheels on, of course!

December was a very busy, exciting and emotional month. We had so many ends to tie up at the mission, so many Christmas Cheer hampers to give out, so many people to farewell, and the final services to conduct in the chapel. We were also flat out on Genesis as we put the finishing touches to our accommodation and amenities.

On 29 December we got word that my stepfather Ernie had passed away in Eildon at the age of seventy. I officiated at his funeral. He and Mum had been married for twelve years, and this had been a providential time for her. She'd had the assistance of a partner through the tough teenage years of the last three children at home. Most of my siblings accepted and respected Ernie, although he probably related more to the boys than the girls, and he was a great mentor and teacher to Ivan.

It was always nice to visit Mum in Eildon, notwithstanding the sad circumstance of this visit. Her home was definitely her castle, although it was the garden around the home that made it so. Mum loved her garden above all, and especially her signature gladioli and tiger lilies. She often walked outside to admire them, but more than that, to gain solace from them, and that was certainly necessary after Ernie's funeral. 'God's creation,' she would call it. I prayed with Mum among the flowers in her garden after Ernie's funeral and there was certainly a sense of peace and tranquillity around.

～

In January 1981 my family and I shifted onto Genesis. It wasn't so bad, because we had plenty of help from members of our former congregation, some of whom planned to be our co-workers. We stored our large items of furniture at John and Jeanette's property in Buninyong, where they would remain until we'd finished building our larger facilities.

It was the hottest January on record in Ballarat. The top temperature for the month was forty-one degrees on 24 January, and the night following was the hottest ever recorded there: the temperature never dropped below twenty-eight degrees. The weather was also very dry. Bev was seven months pregnant, so it was no wonder she was really feeling the heat. She couldn't get much relief other than by putting her feet in a bucket of cold water. We had a dam on the property but it was a fair distance from our caravans—besides, there were a lot of yabbies, and Bev didn't fancy them thinking her feet were a meal!

We had no electricity yet, so there were no fans and certainly no air conditioners. There was only lantern light and candlelight, and no washing machine. I acquired a woodchip heater with a big copper insert to boil the water for both the washing of clothing and the washing of bodies. Chuck would cart water to us from his house in Ballarat, and we would sponge the children and ourselves in a large tin tub. It wasn't easy using a copper to wash all the clothing for a big family and then wringing everything out by hand, but perhaps the hardest part was holding Bev back from doing it all. As many of us who could hopped in and helped. Bev was incredibly stoic and uncomplaining despite the very difficult conditions.

I finally bought a generator to use for lights and a washing machine. We then put in a pipeline to pump water up from the creek to an overhead tank on a stand. I enclosed the tankstand and, hey presto, we had a shower room. All that remained was to heat the water. Another woodchip heater did the trick, and we were in business, luxuriously!

We had worked so hard that March came along in a hurry. Then 2 March was upon us, and our third boy, Mark Andrew, arrived. He missed being born on his sister Christine's birthday by just a few hours. There was great jubilation for the boys as another male joined their ranks, and great joy for the girls who loved mothering their siblings.

~

Following Mark's birth, we spent the next twelve months hectically building the rest of our mudbrick facilities. The local council had been more than happy to approve them. There was a large lounge room and dining room, a bathroom and laundry, a pit toilet, and a big general-purpose shed with a loft and a spare room attached. We placed a pool table in the shed.

Once we were pretty settled, my parents-in-law continued their annual visits to us and stayed for some weeks. They loved living in the mudbrick facilities, and while Bev's mum cooked great cakes and biscuits for the kids, and morning and afternoon teas for the workers, Bev's dad assisted us in any work we were doing. He was closer to me than my own dad, so I started calling him 'Dad', and my mother-in-law 'Mum'.

Mum and Dad were great supporters of our family, and they helped us financially with some of our projects. When they realised that the boys and I had cleared all the land for our facilities entirely by axe, they bought us our first chainsaw.

Dad loved playing pool—in fact, he'd managed a pool room in earlier days. He often joined me, Ellis, David, Paul and Christine for very competitive, entertaining games.

During a very hectic year of working on Genesis, Bev and I received some exciting news: we were going to have our seventh baby in May the next year! This was exhilarating for Bev but also very challenging. Mark was only fourteen months old, and our nine hectares suited him to a tee—right from the time he could crawl he would sit at the door crying to be let out so that he could explore and investigate. Meanwhile, Bev was working incessantly to establish a family home. She said that she couldn't remember being so tired and was struggling with this pregnancy more than all the others.

The morning of 10 May 1982 was so cold that our dam froze over. Bev started to have labour pains before dawn, and when they intensified at 5 a.m. I drove her to hospital. Just two hours later, our seventh child was born. Bev and I had looked up the meaning of

'Sarah', which is 'princess', and 'Jane', which is 'God is gracious', and that was what we named her. As the baby of the family she would be treated as a princess, and God had certainly been gracious in ensuring her safe arrival despite how unwell Bev had been. Our youngest was a fiercely independent child from day one, and she changed the spelling of her name to Sara Jayne as soon as she could, although it means exactly the same thing!

Bev was sent home just a few days later but was very unwell and had to go back into hospital. She'd been suffering from quite severe toxaemia but recovered well.

People have often said to Bev, 'What, seven children? How did you cope?'

She would say, 'I always planned to have four, two boys and two girls, which I did have. But then I wanted one more, and one more, until finally seven. Which of the seven could we have done without, anyway? None of them!'

Bev maintains that 'The thing with large families is that the older ones look after the younger ones, and everyone pulls together. Our family is one of the closest ones I know.'

Since becoming a Christian, I have strongly believed that 'Children are a blessing from the Lord', as the Bible says, and therefore that more children mean more of a blessing. When Sara was born I was overjoyed, yet I felt solemn as well. It was all relatively easy for me. Bev was the one who had to go through all the pain and potential danger. In fact, she was so ill with toxaemia, she could have died.

I have been asked on a number of occasions, 'What makes your marriage strong?' Like every marriage, ours has had its ups and downs, but those times have been like push-ups that have only made us stronger.

When I asked Bev, 'What makes our marriage strong?', she said, 'Because we were called by God to work together, and two are better than one, and our seven children one by one have been the strengthening glue that has helped to keep our marriage together.' That's profoundly true.

To me, strong marriage is about a strong foundation: Jesus. My mother, in her later years, had a saying on her wall: 'Christ is the head of this house'. That needs to be so, but my original idea of marriage was a very chauvinistic one. While Jesus was our spiritual guide, I was the head of everything else in our marriage including managing finances—and I was hopeless at that. Then I read in the Bible that 'There is neither male nor female in Christ', and it was driven home to me that true partnership is not about one person being boss—it is about each spouse contributing according to their strengths. After Bev became our financial manager, we never looked back. I prided myself on being the head, while Bev was the neck that turned the head.

16

The prisoner's friend

I had visited Victorian prisons for many years while I worked with the City Missions in Melbourne and Ballarat. The big news in 1981 was that Prison Fellowship International was coming to Australia that year.

The organisation was founded by Chuck Colson, the former special counsel to President Richard Nixon. In 1974 Chuck had been indicted on charges related to the Watergate scandal—just before this, he'd claimed to be born again. The *Boston Globe* stated, 'If Mr Colson can repent of his sins there just has to be hope for everyone.' He was gaoled for seven months at the Maxwell Federal Penitentiary in Montgomery, Alabama. During his time as an inmate, he saw the need for much reform in both prisons and prisoners. After his release he founded Prison Fellowship International, and Victoria was the first Australian state or territory to commence work with the organisation.

A well-respected man named Reg Worthy was the first State Director. In 1985 he led the first group of Prison Fellowship volunteers, including me, into Ararat Prison. He had conducted a recruiting and training seminar in Ballarat earlier in the year, and I had signed up. We volunteers were given a strong Biblical reminder by Reg before going in. 'Now, don't think you are going in there to convert anyone.'

To me that went down like a lead balloon. *What are we doing here if we aren't here to convert people?* I thought to myself. My brow furrowed with disapproval.

Reg read my body language. 'Something bothering you, Bill?'

'Yes, there is. I disagree that we're not going into prison to convert anyone.'

'Bill!' Reg retorted. 'You didn't hear what I said.'

'Yes, I did. You said, "Don't think you are going in there to convert anyone."'

'Bill, listen again to what I said. I said, "Don't think that *you* are going in there to convert anyone."'

The penny dropped. My role wasn't to convert anyone, it was just to sow and water the seeds of hope. God would do the rest. After twenty years of personal evangelism, the pressure was taken off me: I could now relax and allow my God-given gifts and personality to shine through. Because of that, my next ten years of personal evangelism were to be far more fruitful than the previous twenty. I became a good pool player in prison, and one of my nicknames was 'Bill Subtlecliffe'.

Reg Worthy was undoubtedly the man for the moment to establish the work of Prison Fellowship in Victoria and later to assist in its establishment across Australia. Like me, he had attended the Melbourne Bible Institute and been a youth worker in the Melbourne City Mission. He'd gone on to become a senior social worker in the old Social Welfare Department, and in 1961 he'd become the administrative officer for General Welfare in the Northern Territory. After Reg had investigated the widespread and terrible practice of taking Indigenous children from their parents, which became known as the Stolen Generation, he was involved in both exposing and taking steps to eliminate it.

In 1968 he became the first director of the new Department of Aboriginal Affairs for Victoria, and from there he became the first assistant secretary to the Federal Department of Aboriginal Affairs.

It's no wonder that Reg was held in such high esteem by prison administrators. He opened prison doors that perhaps no other person could have opened. During his fifteen-year role with Prison Fellowship, he was appointed supervisor of all official visitors to Victorian prisons and finally given an Order of Australia Medal for his service to prisons.

Reg was also the one man I couldn't trick with my pranks. On one occasion we were visiting prison together and having a cup of coffee with inmates. When Reg wasn't looking, I put my artificial eye in his cup. The prisoners were beside themselves waiting until Reg drank his coffee down and was confronted with my eye.

To their amazement and mine, he slowly sipped away until he had exposed the eye, which was staring straight at him. He never batted an eyelid. He just put his empty cup down and said, 'You will have to get up earlier in the morning to get me, Bill!'

It brought the house down, and I knew I had a tough act to follow.

~

I was appointed as the senior field officer of Prison Fellowship Victoria. As part of a circuit of all Victorian gaols, I visited Ararat Prison every Friday. I was also the official visitor designated by the state government to hear the complaints of both prisoners and prison officers. Although Ararat Prison was about the same distance from my home in Buninyong as Pentridge Prison in Melbourne, I considered it to be my home prison, and it housed many inmates whom I had visited in Pentridge for a long time before their transfers.

The first time I visited on my own was in 1985, and I didn't get a very warm welcome. In fact, the inmates appeared wary of me, and the atmosphere was tense. Then I arrived at Lennie's cell. After I knocked, he came to the door swiftly and opened it, but he didn't ask me to come in. 'What are you, religious?' he asked aggressively.

'Yes, but . . .'

'Out, get out!' he shouted menacingly as he advanced towards me.

'Hang on . . . How can you order me out when I haven't even come in?' I quipped.

He was taken aback. A smile broke across his face. 'You've got a bit of cheek! I like your style. Do you mean you're not religious?'

'There's good and bad religion. I belong to a practical mob called Prison Fellowship.'

'Oh, come in and tell me about it then.'

When I entered Ararat Prison the next time, it was with two volunteers. We were confronted by an inmate known as 'Big Bad John', the prison's strongman and standover man. Prison officers may have run the gaol, but he ran many prisoners.

'Where do you think you're going?' he bellowed, addressing me as I led the group.

'Visiting around,' I replied.

'Like fucken hell you are!' John thundered. 'You Christians are a pack of fucken wimps! You're not visiting around anywhere.'

Unusual inspiration came to me. Pulling a small New Testament out of my back pocket, I held it out to John.

Still livid, he looked like he was about to snatch it from me.

'How strong are you?' I asked. 'I bet you can't carry this Bible around the prison!'

His huge hand froze mid-motion. He stood stunned and speechless. 'I wouldn't carry that fucken book anywhere!' he finally replied, and stormed off, waving his arms fervently and cursing as he went, but observed by many prisoners and some prison officers.

He'd lost his challenge and given up ground, so we had freedom to move around all the cells without opposition from then on. Behind the scenes, we were applauded by many inmates who had probably been victims of his standover tactics.

Prison culture has its own norms, rules and etiquette. It is said that an Englishman's home is his castle, and so is a prisoner's cell. Visitors need to respect that. After accepting an invitation to enter a particular cell, I couldn't help but notice a grotesque 'work of art' sitting on a small table in the middle of the room. It was a tall bird's-nest construction crisscrossed with sticks and strips of plastic and paper, all perched loosely and precariously. 'What on earth is it?' I asked one of the inmates.

'It's a "gig-trap",' was the answer. 'Stay around and watch it work.'

I didn't have to wait long before another religious visitor turned up. Unlike me, he walked in without even the courtesy of 'May I enter?' His body language was animated as he went straight to the gig-trap and looked at it quizzically—and touched it!

Down it came! Its pieces scattered everywhere. There was a look of stunned surprise on the gig-springer's face.

'Got ya!' came a chorus of prisoners' voices. The 'gig' or 'sticky-beak' had been trapped beautifully.

Prison has a language of its own. Let me illustrate. A well-meaning minister was visiting some prisoners in a cell where I was visiting one day. As he was about to leave, he said, 'Oh well, I must choof off now.' Body language flashed around the room. What he had said in prison language was, 'Oh well, I must go and smoke some marijuana now.' Another time, a visitor entered a cell in my presence and asked, 'Do you mind if I plonk myself down here?' On this occasion, the inmates shared horrified as well as amused looks. The ignorant visitor had actually asked, 'Do you mind if I have sex with one of you?'

~

Within the prison complex in the inner Melbourne suburb of Coburg, there were two gaols: Pentridge proper on the north side, and the Metropolitan Reception Prison on the south. J Division was on the north side. It originally housed juvenile offenders hence the 'J', and then long-term prisoners with good behaviour records, which was the case now.

A tall, wide iron gate separated the two prisons, and a guard tower hovered over the gate. Despite the fact that Pentridge had been in existence for 150 years, it amused me that it still had an archaic security practice. I called it 'the rope, the key and the can trick'. When you arrived at the gate, you called out, 'Gate up!' This didn't really mean the gate would go up—it meant you were to push the gate conventionally to open it. That is, after you carried out the ancient rope, key and can trick!

When the prison officer in the guard tower sighted you and observed your pass affixed to your clothing, he lowered a rope with a tin can on the end. There was a key in the can. You extracted the key, unlocked the gate, opened it and walked through to the other side, closing it after you, all the while being careful not to let go of the rope. If you did, I can tell you from personal experience that it would swing away from you like Tarzan's vine, and you'd have to go through the whole procedure again, to the non-amusement of the officer above! Once you'd completed the exercise, you called out, 'Can up!'

One day I had just executed the trick and gone into a cell in J Division. All of a sudden my inmate host Colin exclaimed, 'Bill, come to the window! The ducks are back!' He excitedly showed me two teal ducks swimming around in the prison pool. Then he told me of their arrival the year before. 'They appeared just like they did today,' he said. 'Mother Duck and Father Duck waddled up to the gate with a brood of ducklings. To everyone's amazement, they waited until a prison officer opened the gate and allowed them to waddle through in single file to the swimming pool. They took over the pool and became our ducks. Woe betide anyone who tried to hurt them. One prisoner was tempted and was quickly told, "If you wring their necks you will get yours wrung!'" He wasn't joking.

It was a great privilege to enter Pentridge as the senior field officer and be able to move around everywhere that inmates worked and lived. It was also a further rich cultural experience. As I entered the industrial area in B Division, heads lifted up everywhere, eyes slowly scanning me. One set of eyes caught my attention as they looked me up and down. They belonged to a stereotypical prisoner: he had a bald head, a barrel chest, bare arms with bulging biceps, many tattoos, and a flowing beard.

'Over here!' he ordered rather than asked. 'Join us for a brew-up.'

At his command, a group of prisoners sat down at a chipped and stained table. A small, sharp-nosed man busied himself making mugs of coffee. My self-appointed host was handed his drink. All the prisoners had a mug in hand. Despite my being commanded to join them, there wasn't a mug for me.

He read my mind. 'My mug's your mug,' he announced.

How thoughtful, I didn't think! His mug looked like it hadn't been washed for years.

He took a big slurp, gave a big burp and—with coffee and saliva dribbling over the rim—handed the mug to me. 'Your turn.'

This was at the outset of the AIDS epidemic, and there was a lot of ignorance about how you could catch it. Thoughts of the virus on the edge of the mug flashed through my mind.

'Have a man-sized swig!' the man bellowed. He sucked a huge amount of coffee out of the mug, then dribbled a large percentage of it from his mouth onto his beard. Sieving the coffee through the hair, he caught it adeptly with his mug at the bottom—then passed the mug to me!

I steeled myself and drank the contents without batting an eyelid, despite what I was thinking inside.

'You're all right,' he said, slapping me on the shoulder.

I had passed the initiation test, and the prison 'tribal chief' had accepted me. Because he did, the other prisoners had to also. It was just before Christmas, and the chief asked me for a Bible and one for each of his mates. They had no say in it!

The tribal chief was ultimately transferred to Ararat Prison. His endorsement of me meant I was widely accepted by prisoners there too.

~

On 4 November 1986, Chuck Colson paid us a visit at Ararat Prison. We'd arranged for him to make a speech, which most of the inmates attended. He kept his audience spellbound with a masterly address on 'The Prisoner Jesus', emphasising that although Jesus was innocent, the rest of us have broken the law in some way or other even if we've never been caught, yet despite that there is hope. Following this speech, Bev coordinated a barbecue for everyone. Later on I received a letter from a prisoner who said he represented all the inmates who were present that day. He expressed deep appreciation for Bev's superb catering and Chuck's very powerful, pertinent address.

The large gathering was the fruit of much practical personal evangelism. When I'd started working with Prison Fellowship, attendance at our functions was very poor. So I decided to try rubbing shoulders with prisoners, particularly through sport, playing pool, tennis and cricket with them. I joined the football team and played alongside them, and I organised an end-of-season presentation night for best and fairest players, who received donated trophies. Because of these efforts, things changed. Word went around: 'Bill and Prison Fellowship have put in for us, so let's put in for them.'

I couldn't have done all this without Bev. She had not only helped me to turn my life around, but she'd also stood shoulder to shoulder with me in a lot of cliff-edge work.

In 1987 we celebrated our twentieth wedding anniversary, and I was conscious that during every one of those years, Bev had shared our marital home with someone in need. Mostly they had been recovering alcoholics and ex-prisoners, but periodically there had been a victim of domestic violence. During that same year we also celebrated Christine going to university, the first of our children to do so. She commenced at Deakin University Geelong Campus to do a BA with a journalism major. Although she lived on campus, with Buninyong just eighty kilometres away, she was still able to come home regularly.

Now, finally, our new house was being constructed, and soon we would have a family home to ourselves. It was a steel-framed kit house with four bedrooms, and we planned to add another three later. I organised a working bee to put the house together like a giant Meccano set. Twenty of us—Prison Fellowship workers, Bev and I, our kids, Chuck Mendenhall and his wife Margaret, and John and Jeanette Lowe—assembled it in a day.

We hoped it wouldn't take long for the finishing touches to be made and for us to move in, freeing up our caravans and mudbrick rooms for people in need to have to themselves. Unfortunately we weren't able to shift into the house for an inordinate amount of time because there was a delay in connecting the electricity, which had to be brought a considerable distance across a dairy farm.

~

In early 1988 Chuck was to have a heartbreaking experience. His wife Margaret was doing some pruning in her garden and had a major heart attack and had to be hospitalised. Bev's parents had recently made their annual pilgrimage to visit us, and Bev had just returned from assisting her dad to drive back to Queensland. Margaret seemed to be recovering well but was worried whether she'd be able to cope with the housework when she was discharged. Bev visited her and assured her that she would take it in hand. The following day Bev was shocked to receive a phone call to notify her that Margaret had suffered another major heart-attack and had died. Chuck was devastated—they had been married for thirteen years. I jointly officiated at Margaret's funeral with the minister of the church that Chuck and Margaret had been attending. Chuck continued living in his married home in Ballarat while assisting at Genesis whenever he could.

In May 1989 it was go, go, go for me in preparation for a trip to Costa Rica, where a Prison Fellowship conference would be held in June. On my last day at Ararat Prison before the trip, an inmate presented me with a beautifully crafted leather wallet that he had made for me to take on the trip. He had embossed the words 'Beloved Bird's Beak' on the front; I had to think for a moment to realise that this meant 'Bill'! I was quite moved.

I was fortunate to have been invited to the conference with Reg Worthy and delegates from all across Australia. Quite remarkably, although Prison Fellowship International was only thirteen years old, it had affiliates in well over fifty countries, and representatives from most of them were able to travel to Costa Rica.

After the conference I said au revoir to Reg and began a whistle-stop tour of a number of American prisons from Florida to California. I was grateful to stay in the homes of my US counterparts. At a gaol in Alabama I had one of the most moving experiences of my life.

The manager was showing me around when someone came up to him and passed on a message from a prisoner on death row. This inmate had heard that a worker with Prison Fellowship was visiting from Australia, and he'd asked if I could visit him at his cell. After the manager agreed, he informed me that the condemned man was a model inmate and a great mentor to younger prisoners. He was only twenty-eight and had been on death row for eight years. He had just exhausted his last appeal, and he was due to be executed by electric chair the next day.

When I spoke to the condemned man through the bars of his cell, he was clearly very saddened by his situation. I found it amazing that this relatively young man, facing certain death very soon, was so sensitive and thoughtful. He asked me about my wife and family. He asked me about Australia, and he asked me about my work in Australian prisons.

Then he shared his testimony with me of becoming a Christian on death row. He had come to realise that in all his early years of running with a gang, he'd never had a true life, just a misguided, violent existence. It had taken a brutal crime to wake him up to that reality, and through the witness of other Christian prisoners he had become a Christian.

He asked if I could take Communion with him and give a Communion talk, and I agreed. We used a polystyrene cup of coffee and a slice of bread as the emblems. The bread represented the body of Jesus, who suffered temporarily so that we wouldn't have to suffer eternally. The coffee represented His blood, which symbolically cleansed us and forgave us of any wrongdoing, and gave us grace to forgive those who may have wronged us. It struck me—and I said this to my companion—that here was an African-American sharing Communion with a white Australian, and the blood of Jesus, the condemned man's blood and my blood were the same colour. We were Christian brothers. We were one.

The condemned man had shaved his head in preparation for the electrodes to go on. 'To preserve my last dignity,' he told me.

And then he gave thanks. Through the bars, he placed his hands on my shoulders and thanked God for all his circumstances, including his death, and for me and my work and my family. He prayed that the rest of my trip would go well and for my safe trip home.

I was quite emotional as a result. He put his arms around me as best he could, and comforted me. A man who was about to die. Then I prayed for him.

Just before I left, I pointed upwards and said, 'We'll meet again.' As I walked away, I looked into the face of faith and courage personified.

That Friday I learnt that he had been executed. I flew back into Australia the following week and had a fax waiting for me at home from the prison manager, which read, 'He was as courageous in dying as he was in living.'

~

I got into an interesting conversation on the flight back to Melbourne. Sitting around me were a fascinating collection of people; among them was a psychologist, a criminologist and a policeman. One of the group raised the topic of 'burnout'. I must say at that stage I had never heard the term, other than in relation to doing burnouts in cars.

One by one we shared our knowledge and experience of burn-out. My companions related frightening tales and statistics of people getting worn out and run down, and experiencing breakdowns in all sorts of ways—in health, in relationships, at work, in business, and in life generally.

Then it was my turn. 'What about you, Bill?'

Apparently the field of prison work was statistically one of the worst for burnout. Yet, as I said, I'd never heard of it. I'd certainly never experienced it.

'Why do you think you haven't experienced burnout?' one of them asked me.

A number of factors came to mind. 'I don't take myself too seriously. I thoroughly enjoy my work and life generally. I tell jokes and have some good belly laughs. I have some great outlets, like prayer and debriefing with my wife and colleagues. Hobbies such as lapidary work and art and craft. Gold-panning with family. And running, which is a tremendous outlet for me because I mostly do it early in the morning without distractions.'

Our discussion was rich and informative, and at the end of it I felt so fortunate that I hadn't experienced burnout.

~

I spent the next week catching up at work, where there was a lot of interest in my trip. The following week was very different. Can you imagine walking into prison after prison for a week with an eye-patch on, and being constantly asked by prisoners and prison officers, 'What happened to your eye?' Then seeing the look on their faces when you answered, 'A dog ran away with my eye.'

Many people take their teeth out overnight. I sometimes take my eye out and sit it on my bedside table. When I did so on this occasion, our chihuahua Prince ran away with it and left it in parts unknown. An ex-prisoner had given Prince to us, and I should have called him 'Prince II' as the successor to my first Prince.

This incident became a great test of whether prayer can really be answered. During the week I told people in prison that God knew exactly where my eye was and would show me. Finally, on the last day of the week, I was visiting Fairlea women's prison when an inmate challenged me: 'Why hasn't God shown you where the eye is yet?' I was conscious of having to visit the prisons again next week and being faced with the same question.

At the weekend I went into the bush near our home and had a long time of fervent prayer. There was no voice from the sky telling me where the eye was, or a picture drawn with clouds showing this to me, but I had great peace that God would somehow help me locate my eye, so I spent the rest of the day cutting firewood.

As evening approached, however, my faith was faltering. I was coming down with a heavy cold and feeling miserable. Doubts and fears flooded my mind, and I was thinking of the humiliation of next week, when I would have to tell the prisoners that God hadn't shown me where my eye was.

It was almost dark, and I was just about to finish cutting firewood and go home, when suddenly, through the roar of the chainsaw, I heard a distinct inner voice telling me that Prince had buried my eye. A clear vision showed me that it was in a garden bed right in front of our house.

Oblivious to my cold, I rushed up the hill to the house, raced inside to get a torch, and told Bev at a pace ten to the dozen what had happened. But she disillusioned me—she'd thought Prince may have buried my eye in that part of the garden, so she'd dug up every bit of it, and the eye wasn't there!

Stuffed up with my cold, I went to bed bewildered but too foggy in the mind to give it more thought. Early next morning I was woken by exactly the same words and vision. I shared this with Bev, and she kindly went out to the same spot in the garden and dug a little bit deeper. There it was.

17

The best and the worst

It was a couple of years after Ernie's death when Mum ventured down to Genesis to visit us again. Ivan brought her. We were still living in our caravans and mudbrick facilities, and she loved them. Like it did for most people her age, including Bev's parents, our lifestyle took her down memory lane to her own childhood and teenage years in rural Victoria. In that era it wasn't uncommon for people to renovate and build their own homes, often using natural resources such as bush timber and mud.

Mum was a bit lonely and lost, although she still had five of her children in Eildon to keep her company, and a sister and two nephews just down the road at Alexandra. Mum was never lethargic, though; she was a keen gardener, and that kept her ever active and interested, particularly looking after her signature gladioli.

She re-engaged with the Salvation Army, which meant she started wearing their uniform with pride, distributing *War Cry* magazines around town, and collecting for their appeals. Having a good cause gave her great motivation, and it took away her loneliness, replacing it with the joy of knowing she was helping others.

Mum also became a letter writer for Prison Fellowship, corresponding with a number of inmates. Sometimes she potentially put herself at risk, but she was oblivious to that. Fortunately I knew the prisoners and could monitor the situation.

Meanwhile, I had recently got back in touch with my biological father, Bob Turner, after some ten years with no contact. Unbeknown to us, some considerable time after Val and I had located him in 1969, he had married a lovely woman named Cath, who brought great happiness and balance into his life. She was a very positive influence on Dad and he travelled extensively with her, going overseas for the one and only time in his life. It was actually Cath who tracked Bev and me down, after which Bev and I and our children, and then Val independently, visited Dad and Cath. Cath was very welcoming.

When Cath died suddenly, her children wouldn't allow Dad to stay in the home he had shared with her, as it was their inheritance. He was devastated and reverted to his heavy drinking. He shifted without letting us know his new address, and it took me some time to track him down again.

To my surprise I had been driving past his door every week as I visited Fairlea women's prison in an outer suburb of Melbourne. I resumed visiting him, and he slowly began to thaw out. Ultimately he introduced me proudly to his neighbours as his son, despite my different surname and my religion.

~

After Chuck's wife Margaret passed away, Chuck was feeling very isolated, and believed he should sell his house in Ballarat and place a relocatable home on Genesis and live there. This corresponded with our belief that we should provide a special-purpose house on our property to accommodate and mentor alcoholics, and ex-prisoners. Chuck was keen on the idea that he could share a house and be supervisor of those we were already working with, so he decided to go ahead with it. However, a major problem presented itself. Because Genesis was in a green belt and had very low-density housing, we had to obtain a special permit from the council in order to place a second house on it. We had to advertise our intentions and allow residents the opportunity to object. After convening a meeting with them, the majority were satisfied with our safeguards and we were granted a permit in 1990. The good thing was that after we shifted into our new house and placed our relocatable accommodation, we retained our caravans and annexes to be used for emergency facilities. And, just as importantly, Bev's parents were able to stay in them on their annual visits.

I had recently been appointed by the Minister for Corrections as Official Visitor to the new medium-security Loddon Prison in Castlemaine. My role was to hear the complaints of prisoners and prison officers and to report to the minister. I was also to work there as the Prison Fellowship Senior Field Officer. I had prayed much about the prospects of being involved with a prison from its inception, as I hoped this would allow me to implement programs of the greatest benefit there. Now this opportunity had arrived.

Loddon was duly opened in August 1990, and I was at hand to welcome bus loads of prisoners, many of whom I knew, as they arrived from Pentridge. Being able to hear and respond to concerns from prisoners and prison officers was one way to be of assistance and to establish rapport; having the right to move around the entire prison and meet with inmates in groups or one on one was a real privilege. One on one was my specialty.

Towards the end of that very busy year, Reg Worthy contacted me with a special request. Prison Fellowship had shifted its office from the north-eastern suburb of Ivanhoe to the outer-eastern suburb of Ringwood. The Ivanhoe office had been attached to Allan Moore Lodge, which accommodated a number of ex-prisoners. The lodge was to be closed with the relocation of the office to Ringwood. Reg asked me if Genesis would name the extra house Allan Moore Lodge, and consider accepting any further referrals. We agreed.

As Chuck was already living in the house, it was decided he would be the in-house supervisor. He had been involved with many ex-prisoners while living in the Hostel at the Men's Centre in Melbourne and through being a volunteer with the Ballarat City Mission. Never to give much away, when I asked Chuck how he felt about his new role, he nonchalantly answered, 'I served in Korea'. He was quite excited nevertheless at the prospect of mentoring the new residents.

Following that, the Office of Corrections told me that they were having some difficulty releasing a few Governor's Pleasure (GP) prisoners, and were wondering if I could assist them. These prisoners had served the sentence originally given them but were still considered a major risk to the community if released. They were kept in prison until the state governor, with advice, deemed it was safe for them to be released. Some had already been imprisoned for over twenty years.

The proposition was that such prisoners would be given twelve months of extended leave to live in the new Allan Moore Lodge on our property. I would be responsible for their security and their pre-release programs, and their integration into the community. If at the end of twelve months it was considered that they had satis-factorily integrated into the community, they would be released. In consultation with Bev and our children and co-workers, and after much prayer, I said yes.

All who were selected were well known to me, and I was satis-fied that they were able to be rehabilitated. Bev had visited them with me in prison also, and was comfortable with them coming to live on Genesis. There were to be no sex offenders.

One GP prisoner joined our family for Christmas lunch in 1990. Can you imagine not having Christmas lunch with your loved ones for twenty years? Not seeing a Christmas tree with presents under it for all those years? Never giving or receiving a Christmas present outside prison during that time? Not being able to participate in any religious or other festivity with your loved ones for twenty years?

Our guest had been released into our care sometime before Christmas and was as excited as a little child. 'What gifts should I get? Where should I get them? Can you come with me and help me get them, Bev?' However much he paid for the presents would be worth it—after all, he had many years to make up for. 'The greatest joy of all for me was to be free to see and feel the Christmas Spirit out of prison,' he said.

Things that we are perhaps most cynical about—or take for granted—were the most special to him. Things like Christmas carols playing in shopping centres, and decorations dressing up drab city streets. Christmas advertising pamphlets, which we might call 'junk mail', were relished by him. All of these things were of great significance to one who had not experienced Christmas day outside prison for so long.

The lunch was something else. His eyes sparkled with absolute joy to see the table decked out with bowls of nibbles and colourful bonbons. And there was a novel table centrepiece made by Bev: a large bottle of soft drink covered with light mesh and coloured tinsel, with numerous sweets attached to it like fruit on a tree.

Tears welled up in our guest's eyes. He pulled a bonbon with me, then donned the festive paper hat excitedly. It was the food, however, that brought a perpetual smile to his face: a lavish smorgasbord of turkey, chicken, ham and pork, including crackling, with rich gravy and apple sauce, and a wonderful array of roast vegetables, followed by traditional plum pudding and custard, with cream and ice-cream. All had been prepared and cooked by Bev and the family. Our guest said that he felt overwhelmed with gratitude for being set free temporarily and allowed to enjoy such a wonderful Christmas lunch with our family.

But I was most moved by what he told me in private after lunch. He had killed someone horrifically, and he said that although he now knew, as a Christian convert, that he had been forgiven by God, he still felt very sad and guilty. He kept thinking of how the person he had killed hadn't had a Christmas lunch since that fateful day either, and never would—and that every year, Christmas was marred for his family and friends by the realisation that he had been killed just after Christmas.

~

At the same time that we were welcoming ex-prisoners onto Genesis, I continued to come up with new ways to reach people who were still in prison. Having been a member of the Ballarat Speaker's Club in the early 1970s, I was well aware of the worth of speaking and debating clubs. They gave confidence, self-esteem and self-discipline to participants. My thoughts were that the clubs would be ideal subtle diversion programs also, enabling prisoners to bring their anger under control subconsciously. Prisoners generally were very competitive, and because they could lose points in a debate for losing their temper, I was sure they would try their best to become disciplined enough to win. So I sought permission to form a speaking and debating club at Loddon. Convinced of the worth of these clubs, the governor and the programs manager readily gave approval. Ellis and a friend of ours—both members at the church where our family attended—became great volunteers for me in the club.

Speaking and debating clubs could also give spiritual bonuses. Harry's experience was one such case. A Loddon inmate, Harry came along to one of our Speaker's Club meetings initially for a laugh and to disrupt us. Many of his mates, however, were taking it seriously and loving it. Harry finally took the attitude of 'if you can't beat them, join them' and became a keen participant in the club. He was a chronic drug addict, and his involvement in the club was to be the impetus for a life-changing experience.

By 1991, the year after Loddon opened, our Speaker's Club had become very good. I had brought in a number of male debating teams to compete against them, and Loddon were undefeated. Harry was by then an extremely good speaker and debater; in fact, he'd become the club's champion for major debates. I should mention that I'd also commenced a Speaker's Club at the Tarrengower women's prison in Maldon, and whenever I took over a team from Loddon, the women defeated the men.

I talked up the reputation of Loddon's club enough to get the Ballarat Toastmasters debating team interested in pitting themselves against them. They accepted an invitation to a debate at Loddon. Toastmasters has been around since the early thirties. It started in the Young Men's Christian Association (YMCA) in the US, and was designed to teach people how to speak effectively, plan programs, and to work on committees. It later included competitive debating. The topic of the Ballarat Toastmasters/Loddon Prison debate was Karl Marx's statement that 'Religion is the opiate of the masses'. Prisoners flocked to the event.

Harry was the final speaker on the affirmative side and gave a brilliant defence. 'The atheist Karl Marx tried to deride religion by saying that the majority of people are controlled by religion, like the drug opium, which is bad. But there are helpful drugs as well as harmful drugs. Even if religion is the drug of the masses, is that necessarily a bad thing? Religion has implemented many good and integral parts of society, such as nursing services, hospitals and pensions.'

Harry wore his heart on his sleeve in an impassioned final proposition. 'I'm a junkie—I've been hooked on heroin and many other drugs. I've been so desperate for a fix that I've committed crimes that have put me in prison and cost me not just my liberty but my loved ones, everything but my life, and almost my life many times. What if God is real and is the spiritual opiate of the people? A good drug? The ultimate fix? Would that be a bad thing?'

The Loddon team won the debate, and the chairman of the adjudicating panel declared that this was no mean feat. The Ballarat team were the reigning Victorian Toastmasters Debating Champions.

Later Harry realised that he had nothing to lose by trying the ultimate fix himself. He said that he'd got 'hooked on God', and that he had never been so satisfied, fulfilled and rational at the same time.

~

After a couple of full-on years at work, I took on a different sort of challenge: I chose to celebrate my fiftieth birthday, 5 April 1993, with a parachute jump. As part of a New Year's resolution, I had decided that from my half century on, every five or ten years I would celebrate my birthday in a very challenging way.

I completed an all-day training course at the Meredith Parachute Club between Ballarat and the city of Geelong, and I was due to have my first jump a week later. The course had been very thorough and reassuring, and I was pumped and primed to go.

On the day I requested to go in the first load of jumpers and to be the first to jump. Led by me, the group were lined up at the railing in front of the hangar, our parachutes strapped on. We were instructed to pretend to pull the ripcord in practice for the real thing—not that we would have to pull the ripcord for our first jump. We would be connected to a static line, which would automatically pull our ripcord.

'Okay,' said the instructor, 'on the count of three, pretend to pull the ripcord. One, two, three, pull!'

And pull I did—not in pretence but the real thing.

'Oh no!' the instructor called out.

My parachute opened up as fast as a rocket. Had there been any wind about, I may have taken off. The instructor rushed to grab my chute and, with a couple of other pairs of hands helping him, pulled it down and then gathered it in. 'You know what this means, don't you, Bill? You'll miss the first load while we repack your chute!'

I was as deflated as the parachute now. Maybe I was just a little bit nervous! It didn't deter me, though: I was just as keen to jump with the next load.

'Still jumping first, Bill?'

'Yes.'

The plane seemed to be slow at climbing to the jump height of 3000 feet, but we were finally there. 'Start to get ready Bill. I'll hook you up. Over to the edge. Sit down in the doorway. Legs over the edge. Arch your back and throw your hands back as you jump. Then brace yourself for the chute opening. One, two, three, go!'

Some words came to my mind from the Bible, 'Underneath are the everlasting arms', and I was absolutely calm as I jumped.

The chute opened almost on cue, jerking me up exactly as described. *How exhilarating!* I thought. *What a view.* It was only three thousand feet down, and I was dropping at over 124 miles an hour, but it didn't feel like it. Helmet and goggles minimised the impact of the wind. Bird orientated as I was, I thought it was a bird's-eye view. The airfield wasn't far from Merideth township and the Ballarat–Geelong Road. Cyprus trees lined the road. I could see some cattle grazing, oblivious to me, obviously used to this. It all looked like a large Lego scene that I was holding a magnifying glass to.

The ground was coming up fast. I could see someone waving batons near the target, guiding me there. Then I saw a group of people. They're looking up at me. It's Bev and the kids. I pulled on the cords, and the parachute tilted back and created drag, slowing remarkably. *Hooray, I'm going to hit the bullseye! Whoops, I've overshot, but just by two or three metres. Not bad.*

The chute fluttered down behind me, to be grabbed by the target marshal. I stumbled a little and fell onto my knees, then I got to my feet and threw my arms up in triumph and exhilaration.

My birthday jump wasn't the only reason that 1993 had started off on a high note. Ron Nikkel, the president of Prison Fellowship International, was scheduled to pay us a visit from America. His mission was to formally recognise the enormous contribution of Reg Worthy to Prison Fellowship Victoria. Reg planned to retire at the end of June.

The Prison Fellowship council of management had been seeking a replacement for Reg over many months, to no avail. Meanwhile, many Prison Fellowship volunteers had been urging me to apply for the position. Just days before the scheduled meeting with Ron Nikkel, I became convinced that I should put myself forward.

At the meeting on 6 June, as a great surprise and with much joy, I was commissioned as executive director of Prison Fellowship Victoria. Management were unanimous in their belief that I was the right choice. Three hundred people were present, and many prison workers told me later that had they known my commissioning was going to occur, they would have been present also. I'd been visiting prisons for twenty-eight years and was thrilled to the back teeth with this development. While I was extremely humbled, I also felt that I was born for the moment—or should I say 'reborn'? It seemed a natural progression for me after I had served a long apprenticeship. Over nearly a decade, Reg and I had built an incredible working relationship, and he had taught me so much.

I had to be up and running in my new role, because a state conference needed to be planned for the end of October. I put in the hard yards, and it all worked out. The headline on an article about the conference read, 'STATE CONFERENCE GREAT SUCCESS'. And it was. A hundred and twenty volunteers and supporters were present, with senior prison officials and officers and serving prisoners participating. All attested to the great work being done by Prison Fellowship in Victorian prisons. I was pretty proud and buoyed to be building on the success of my predecessor and that the staff and volunteer morale was so high.

By the end of the year, though, I was pretty exhausted after such a heavy workload in my new role, but I knew it was all worth-while when I received these words from Reg on a Christmas card: 'Dear Bill, your appointment is the climax of years of prayerful pleas to the Almighty for a worthy successor. You fit the "Bill"! With every blessing and expectation of hearing a constant song of angels during the coming year, your brother in Christ, Reg.'

But after that, things changed. Reg's attitude to me changed. He had doubts that I could manage the admin work and was frequently critical of my efforts. I was bewildered. Although economic times were tough, and the government had cut funding for the sector, Prison Fellowship was doing very well. Our donations had increased, and morale was high among staff and volunteers. It was a wonder I could manage anything, however: management hadn't replaced my role as field officer, so I was still responsible for visiting prisons regularly as well as being the state director.

Over the next six months it became obvious that I was just the token director. After Reg's retirement he'd remained on the council of management and had influence there. I likened it to a church minister retiring but then staying on the board and interfering with the new minister's role. I met with Reg and told him this a number of times; each time he apologised, saying it was hard for him to let go of the reins. Things would be fine for a while, then another incident would occur.

The bottom had dropped out of my world. It seemed that all of a sudden I had gone from being the golden-haired boy to the awful ogre. 'What has gone wrong, Lord?' I cried out. 'You promised you had given me an open door that no one could shut—and yet the door is being slammed in my face!' I'd thought I had used up all my tears during my years of abuse, but now I regularly woke myself and Bev up sobbing.

Every week I was driving, misty-eyed and tired, to my office in Melbourne and around to prisons and back home, yet I couldn't break confidence about what was going on. As I hadn't done for years, I bottled things up. It was taking its toll. I was hardly sleeping and driving dangerously. Bev told me a number of times, 'Bill, you've got to resign from Prison Fellowship. Things are not going to change, and the load will kill you if you don't.'

At first this seemed extreme. But when I went to sleep behind the wheel at a red light in Melbourne, then soon after fell asleep on a country road between prisons and nearly ran into a tree, this drove home to me the seriousness of my situation. Finally, after much prayer and consultation with Bev, it became clear that my position was untenable.

My letter of resignation is dated 20 June 1994, just a year and a fortnight after my commissioning. Part of the letter states, 'My nine and a half years with Prison Fellowship have been the most fruitful of my 27-year ministry. I have enjoyed rich fellowship and service with the Prison Fellowship Family, including especially yourself, Reg . . .'

Writing it broke my heart. I was shattered.

The days after my resignation were a blur. Bev told me that she had never seen me so down. She would come home from her job as a church administrator to find me still sitting at the kitchen table, head in hands and sometimes just staring into space.

This was totally out of character for me, but it didn't last long. I had Bev, our children, our Genesis associates and fellow churchgoers, and especially the Lord to unload on and to draw encouragement and inspiration from. Many prisoners, ex-prisoners, and Prison Fellowship workers and supporters encouraged me greatly also.

18

Joy and sadness

Following my resignation I had a considerable interlude from prison work, which proved to be very providential. By the end of the year, with volunteer assistance, I'd completed the three-bedroom extension to our home with a bathroom and kitchenette. We now had a self-contained unit to accommodate any visiting family members or friends. Ellis again did the plumbing work on the extension.

This interlude also afforded me the opportunity to catch up with our neighbours David and Lea Senior, who lived at the top of our lane. Since our move to Genesis we'd all become good friends, and David had become a Prison Fellowship volunteer. Knowing my situation, he asked if I would like a job at his Antiques and Collectables Centre in Ballarat, the largest such business in western Victoria. I took up the offer, and it was a steep learning curve for me; I was pretty experienced with collectables but very inexperienced with antiques. As well as feeling that I was chaplain to the business, I considered myself to be chaplain to the Ballarat second-hand trade as a whole. I counselled many customers for grief, loss and stress, and I officiated at a number of their weddings and funerals.

While working at the antique centre I received the most shocking and distressing phone call that I'd ever had. It was 13 September 1996, and it was to inform me that my younger brother Gordon had just died in a tragic road accident. He was a married man with four children and was only forty-eight. I couldn't answer the questions, 'Are you alright Bill? Was it bad news?' I withdrew to find some solitude in a back room and cried my eyes out. I was devastated. We had a special bond, partly over sport, and a similar mischievous personality and smile. He was a great husband and father as well as an excellent Australian Rules football player and coach. In the extreme busyness of both our lives we never saw a lot of each other, but when we did, the lack of quantity of time spent together was made up with quality of time. We absolutely loved and enjoyed being in one another's company.

In 1998, I was invited back into official religious work when the Colac Church of Christ asked me to be their pastor. Colac is a small town about an hour's drive from Buninyong. Bev would be on the board of management with me, and that was very appealing. It's strange to say that it reminded us of our joint City Mission roles. We would remain living on Genesis and commute to Colac.

It's probably terrible to say, but when I heard Colac the first thing I thought was *Wow, the home of Cliffy Young and the Six-Day Race*. Bev nudged me at this point after reading my mind and said, 'Bill, there're more important things!' And of course there were. Colac was home to a beautiful little rural church with a very warm-hearted but tiny congregation that was struggling and urgently needed encouragement, guidance and vision. The symbols were all around. Lake Colac with its famous pelicans: a symbol of sacrifice in tough times; its prolific dairy-farming industry indicating plenty of milk to spare and share. And it was the gateway to the famous Otway Ranges and the Great Ocean Road. And dare I say as well, if not selfishly, it was the mecca of ultramarathon running! It seemed to me to represent how sacrifice and sharing and endurance could win through and impact many lives in positive ways.

My induction service was in early 1999. I decided to parachute into Colac as close to the church as possible, making a symbolic statement about help coming from on high. But there were a couple of problems with this idea. One was that because I'd only had a limited number of solo parachute jumps, I wasn't qualified to do a solo target jump—I had to do a tandem jump into a school oval near the church.

The second problem was that it ended up being too windy to attempt to parachute into Colac, so the pilot decided to divert the jump to the airport a few kilometres outside town. A lot of friends and visitors were parked around the school oval, waiting for me to come out of the sky. When they were informed that the landing site had changed, they rushed out to the airport—some rushed too fast, unfortunately, and got booked for speeding.

Apart from the wind, it was a glorious late-autumn day for a jump. The temperature was in the high teens on the ground, but a few thousand metres up it was a different world. There was literally ice in the air, and the atmosphere was thick with fog. We plummeted through fluffy white clouds to see a beautiful dairy-farming panorama surrounding the airport. Thanks to my tandem jumper, I had an on-target landing. Symbolism achieved—help arriving from on high!

The locals were mostly very positive about my jump, warming to something done quite unconventionally and symbolically, and a number of them pulled me up in the street to tell me so. But there were a few negative reactions from churchgoers, including a couple of letters to the editor in the local newspaper with comments like 'Christianity is not about grandstanding' and 'Jesus wouldn't have done that'. I couldn't help myself from replying: 'The Bible says Jesus is coming back on a cloud, not too dissimilar to a parachute!'

The church's management decided that our target group would be the unchurched rather than the churched, and our ambience would primarily be seeker-friendly. To that end we established cafe-style decor for our Sunday services: wooden pews were replaced with comfortable padded chairs around small circular tables. Down the back of the church we put tea, instant coffee, milk, sugar and an electric urn of hot water, next to plates filled with plenty of biscuits. Churchgoers could have a hot drink and biscuits while enjoying motivational biblical messages from me and the occasional guest speaker. Between speeches we played a mixture of contemporary and older Christian music.

For primary and secondary schoolkids we commenced a weekly program called Oasis, with motivational messages on DVDs, games, art and craft. Each week it concluded with a superb two-course meal, a great attraction that allowed parents, guardians and grand-parents to be involved in Oasis by preparing and serving the food. Fifty young people attended regularly and enthusiastically.

Outside of church, I soon found a fun way to participate in the community. Colac had an unusual major event every Melbourne Cup Day: the Ferret Cup. I decided to purchase and train a pair of racing ferrets, who I named 'Praise the Lord' and 'Hallelujah'. Neither of them won the cup, but believe it or not, to the great amusement of everyone, Praise the Lord beat a ferret named Satan!

~

For me, a great bonus of our work in Colac was the famous Six-Day Race, an ultramarathon championship held there every November. Cliff Young—or 'Cliffy', as he was affectionately known—had been instrumental in founding the race in 1984. From the tiny town of Beech Forest, just outside Colac, he had established himself in folklore as a 61-year-old gumboot-wearing endurance-running potato farmer by winning the Westfield Sydney to Melbourne Ultramarathon in 1983.

I'd been running ultramarathons since 1973, and the Six-Day Race was my Mecca, as it was for many other Australian and international ultra runners. In my first year in Colac in 1999, I qualified and was accepted into the field. However, a couple of weeks out from the race I twisted my ankle in a pothole while training and suffered a hairline fracture. I hastened to a sports clinic and received electrical stimulation for two weeks to accelerate healing. Against medical advice I started in the race and only managed to run eighty-eight kilometres before having to pull out. Nevertheless, I had achieved my long-held ambition to run in the Six-Day Race.

At the end of 1999, the race looked like it was going to cease. Bev and I convened a public meeting and sought to revive interest in it. We expanded the organising committee, increased the number of volunteers, increased the amount of sponsorship and—all importantly—substantially increased the prizemoney. This attracted the world's greatest ultramarathon runner, Yiannis Kouros, back for only the second time, after he'd established a new world record in the inaugural Six-Day Race. I qualified again, and while Yiannis came first, I ran a respectable 406 kilometres to be the tenth Australian out of fourteen in the field of twenty-three runners.

Because of our keen interest in the Six-Day Race, I was elected race president for 2001 and Bev organising secretary, and we continued the revamp that had started the year before. I ran with injuries again and only managed 122 kilometres. It was to be my last run in the race.

I had many ultramarathon runs before running in the Six-Day Race, most of them for fundraising. One notable one was a Ballarat to Melbourne run when our daughter Sara came along as my handler. Sara was a trained nurse, which was just as well as I thought I might need one. Anne Lane, a friend from our congregation in Colac, also came along. She was a good masseuse, which was going to come in useful. When I reached my destination, I was to deliver a letter to John So, Lord Mayor of Melbourne, from David Vendy, the Mayor of Ballarat, to invite Melbournians to come to the glorious Ballarat Begonia Festival.

The day of the run was quite hot and when I spied a large dam close to the road, the temptation was too great. The farmhouse was just behind the dam so I went and asked the occupants if I could have a swim. They were quite happy for me to do so. I was wearing flesh-coloured lycra tights under my shorts for the run. As I dived into the dam from a steep bank, my shorts came off. My favourite running shorts! I didn't let on at first that I had lost them, assuming they would be easy to find, but they weren't. In fact, I couldn't find them at all. I couldn't believe how deep the dam was—it was so deep I couldn't touch the bottom. I dived in time and time again trying to retrieve my shorts, but in vain. After a bit I realised that I'd taken up too much time and had to get back on the road again. Out of the dam I came—to an audience. The dam owners had come down to see the running contingent, and a journalist had noticed our bus with a banner on it and had come to interview me. I emerged from the dam, dripping wet. Sara let out a gasp. 'Dad!' I looked down to my horror: my clinging lycra flesh-coloured tights made it look like I had nothing on. She threw me a towel to cover up just as the camera man was about to take a photo. Sara still talks about the incident as if her innocence was taken from her that day.

~

In the three years that Bev and I had been commuting between Genesis and Colac, we had been touched by a lot of sadness, as well as some powerful reasons to be grateful.

In June 2000, Bev and I were informed that our loyal friend and long-time associate Jim Bentley had passed away. He'd helped to nurse each of our seven children and become a much-loved member of our family. When he was inebriated, he used to say with slurred speech, 'I love you, Billy!' And he did, but not just me, Bev also, and all of our children.

I owe an enormous amount to Jim. He was an extremely intelligent person who, in different circumstances, could have pursued any career he chose; he regretted that he hadn't furthered his education. I, on the other hand, hadn't seen much need for more academic education personally—after all, I'd had a number of illustrious jobs, including as the state director of Prison Fellowship. Jim had changed my thinking, however. The clincher was an appeal he made right to my heart: 'We need someone like you to go to university, Bill, to show others from our background that we can do it.' It took a while for his message to get through to me, but ultimately it did. I then studied at Deakin University for a BA with a major in literature and obtained more qualifications from two other universities.

Jim's encouraging, loving and challenging role in my life demonstrates how important it is to affirm the potential in people—to inspire them and encourage them and motivate them, not just for their sake but for the sake of everyone they encounter.

Jim went to be with Jesus, whom he loved so much, on 29 June 2000, and I officiated at a celebration service in memory of him. I was thrilled that the word 'Mizpah' was placed on his plaque at the crematorium. I introduced that word to Jim from the Bible, and he loved it. It means, 'May the Lord watch over us while we are absent from each other'.

A few months later I completed the Six-Day Race, a very satisfying but especially exhausting one. Bev had carried a huge load as my handler and manager and as a race committee member; she was just about out on her feet and yet had to drive me all the way home to Buninyong once the race was over. First thing in the morning we drove to Colac for the church service, and following that, of course, we drove home again.

At home we'd hardly had time to relax before I received a phone call from my biological father's doctor. He told me that he had just received Dad's chest X-rays, and unfortunately Dad had extensive and advanced lung cancer. He only had about three months to live. The doctor then asked me if I would deliver the news to Dad. It was a tough call.

When I gave Dad the news, he didn't show much emotion, as was typical for him—he had an old-world, stoic nature. But he then surprised us enormously by asking if he could come and live with us for his remaining days. He wanted to get to know his grandchildren.

We set about packing up his belongings and moving him to Buninyong. It was a very happy time, although very sad and surreal too. In the lounge room Dad held court to our children and grandchildren, to Ellis, to palliative care nurses, and to many of our friends and extended family members. Bev and I were commuting to Colac each weekend, so our daughter Angela and her immediate family, together with other nearby family members, looked after Dad in our absence, and Val came up for an occasional weekend to give them some respite.

The Christmas of the year 2000 is the only one I remember having with my father, and it was wonderful. But although life with Dad had come full circle and we were together again, he had little time to live. And to the end, sadly, although I knew he was my biological father, there was never any bonding. We remained strangers.

The power of forgiveness and acceptance was very real for us, though. Dad never said sorry for anything, and I didn't ask him or need him to, but he knew he was loved and forgiven. He died in peace on 23 February 2001, our son David's birthday, two days short of the three months that Dad's doctor estimated he would live. I officiated at his funeral.

Typical of my life to this point, following the death of my father I was up and running again with a very heavy schedule. I would like to think I'd had adequate time to grieve, but truth be known I probably hadn't.

That year I had another personal pastoral concern when my stepbrother and spiritual brother Ellis became increasingly unwell. He was an amazing survivor—he had survived cancers and heart attacks and a stroke. Now he had a severe lung condition and associated respiratory problems. The specialist who attended him in hospital said, 'I've looked after this man for years, and every time I've seen him it's been for a life-threatening ailment. It's a miracle he's survived.' Ellis went to his heavenly reward on 14 September 2001. I was privileged to take a celebration service for his life.

What an example of the power of love and forgiveness and Christian conversion Ellis was. In 1988 he'd come to live with us and assist us on Genesis—his work there included all the plumbing—and he'd been a volunteer at the Ballarat mission for years before that. He had assisted me in prisons as well.

Ellis was a good mechanic who had once been in the Royal Australian Electrical and Mechanical Engineers in the Regular Army. His skills made him a great mentor for our youngest son, Mark, who had always wanted to create things out of whatever he could lay his hands on. At first this was mainly wood and bark, then I got him an old bike and his own spanners, and he'd sit for hours pulling the bike apart and putting it back together. When Ellis worked with us on Genesis, Mark became his shadow, following him around constantly, observing and questioning and learning.

When Ellis's specialist intimated that he was very low, Mark was able to visit him and thank him for all that he had done for him. Ellis was on a respirator and it wasn't easy for Mark to communicate with him, although he was now twenty.

The passing of Jim, Ellis and my father, in the space of fifteen months, caused me to reflect on my own life. Each man represented in different ways how far we'd all come, and each man gave hope for everyone in similar circumstances. *How blessed we are*, I thought, *to be touched by lives positively and to touch lives positively.* The multiplying effect of that is amazing. My positive interaction with the shopkeeper who caught me shoplifting had set off a chain reaction for me, breaking a negative cycle and starting a positive one. There had been similar moments in Jim's life, and Ellis's, and even my father's.

In my life, what an incredible blessing there has been from Bev and seven children and twenty-one grandchildren and one great-grandchild, plus innumerable others. *I am of all people most blessed*, I thought. *May I continue to pass that blessing on.*

19

The culmination

Although I'd been a risk-taker and lived on the edge all my life, I believed that any risks I took were calculated as long as I could see what they were and took reasonable steps to minimise them. That was my self-justification, anyway! In April 2003, my children thought they had found my Achilles heel. They should have done by my sixtieth year! It was my discomfort at being in the sea and not knowing what was swimming underneath me. They called it fear, while I called it healthy apprehension.

One of my kids said, 'Dad, you need to overcome your fear of sea creatures.' They knew I would play into their hands—that ultimately I'd take up the challenge and endeavour to prove them wrong—so they bought me a Dive with Sharks package at the Melbourne Aquarium. I found that I was really looking forward to it. The closer my sixtieth got the more excited I got.

I headed in early that morning. First I did a four-hour training course that entailed a comprehensive session on scuba diving, then a practice run in an indoor swimming pool, and finally a thorough test and qualification. And then the big moment arrived. I suited up and slipped into a huge tank filled with aqua-blue salt water. I had been assured that all the sharks and other predatory sea creatures had been fed beforehand.

As I reached the bottom of the tank, a huge stingray glided over my head, and I tickled its stomach. (This was three years before Steve Irwin's death from a stingray attack!) I squatted down at the front of the public viewing area while sharks, rays and spectacular tropical fish swam around and over me. I'd known that Bev and the children were coming down to watch me, but I hadn't known that a considerable number of friends and extended family had been invited to watch also. This made the incredible experience extra special.

It was awesome to be in that world of wonders for thirty minutes. I didn't want to get out! I could see what was going on around me and felt no fear. What a birthday present—one of the best.

Afterwards, Bev told me that we'd been invited over to our daughter Pamela's place for an evening cuppa, so we headed straight there. I opened the front door, and as I walked in a loud chorus of 'Happy birthday!' greeted me. The house was packed with well-wishers, including many who hadn't been able to make it to the aquarium. The party capped off a very fulfilling day.

～

It was hard to believe that eight years had passed since my resignation from Prison Fellowship. I had achieved a lot in that time, and recently I'd become a qualified life coach.

Creature of habit that I was, while Dad had been staying with us over Christmas 2000, I'd been very exercised in my mind about what my New Year's resolution and my personal goal for 2001 would be. Then an incredible incident occurred. I was sitting by the creek on our Genesis property, contemplating and praying, when a woman in running gear jogged through our front gate, not realising it was private property. We had a friendly chat, and she told me she was a life coach. I had recently read an advertisement for a life-coaching course. 'What exactly is a life coach?' I asked.

'Well, life coaching, as distinct from mentoring or counselling, is a unique technique that assists people to discover for themselves their untapped potential, and how to achieve it. It can help people from any field, sporting or corporate, white collar or blue collar. Those who have been made redundant, can't find work or are tired of current work can discover new gifts in their lives, then make a career out of them or just enjoy them.'

I asked her where she had trained, and it was at the Life Coaching Academy of Victoria, the same one I'd seen advertised! She said it was believed to be the premier life-coaching academy in Australia. I considered this an answer to my prayer. When I told Bev, she agreed that I should apply to do the course. I did the theoretical part during July 2001, including a weekend intensive with my fellow students, and for the rest of the year I was monitored with mock life-coaching phone sessions. I did an exam and graduated, still unsure where life coaching might lead me.

By 2003 I still couldn't see the purpose of being a life coach. But my drive and ambition weren't diminished, and I retained my commitment to the belief that 'Everything works together for good. There is a purpose in everything that happens.'

Out of the blue, Prison Fellowship Victoria contacted me. There had been two directors in the years since I had resigned, and the latest, having discovered I was a qualified life coach, asked me if I'd be prepared to present a life-coaching module in a new pre-release course called 'Lives in Transition'. It was to be conducted at Barwon maximum security prison, about an hour and a quarter's drive from Buninyong. The course was to commence in September 2003, and although it would be conducted five days a week, I could present my module as part of one day. The Colac church was happy for me to do that, so I said yes.

I was over the moon! Finally the reason I'd been prompted to become a life coach fell into place. And I loved being back in prison. I had a ball, not just presenting the module but also catching up with many prisoner friends. A good friend of mine, Arthur Bolkas, an ex-prisoner who had become a committed Christian with a Master's in criminology, presented a module on 'Restorative Justice'.

In 2004, the director of Prison Fellowship asked me to become the director of Lives in Transition. I agreed on the provision that I could redesign the course, and my proposition was that it should form an alliance with the Gordon Institute of TAFE in Geelong. Lives in Transition would incorporate some of their work-oriented modules such as 'Fork-Lift Operating' and 'Certificate I in Engineering', First Aid and level-2 Food Handling. Arthur's 'Restorative Justice' module would remain as a vital encouragement for accountability and a spiritual component, while my 'Life Coaching' module would continue too.

My proposition was accepted, so I became the course director. Later on I included an art elective that most of the prisoners took up. It was taught by David O'Callaghan, an exceptional artist who had done some of the illustrations for the Chronicles of Narnia film series. When the elective began, I wondered what basic kind of art David would start with. To my surprise, he started by teaching the prisoners to draw portraits, and within a month some of them were turning out reasonable attempts.

The revised Lives in Transition program was so popular with inmates that we couldn't accommodate them all in the ten-week course, so we conducted interviews with prisoners and accepted a maximum of twenty-five per term on the basis of those considered to be most committed to rehabilitation. A mentor was offered for the first year following their release; this was voluntary, but most took it up. For those prisoners who completed the course, reoffending was reduced considerably.

∼

Many people who know John Burt, the former longstanding principal of the Ballarat Specialist School, would be surprised to know we were in prison together. While I was directing Lives in Transition, I invited John in as a guest speaker on a couple of occasions. Then in April 2006, he asked me if I'd be interested in joining the staff at his school as chaplain as well as support worker for students, parents and staff.

I needed time to consult with Bev and God about this and both were in favour of it so I said 'yes'. When I left prison work in 2006 it was very timely for me. I had been visiting prisons and working in prisons since 1965. I likened that to rescuing people who had fallen off cliffs and helping them recover. It was now high time to spend more time preventing people, especially young people, from falling off cliffs in the first place. Bev and I would continue pastoring the Colac Church on weekends only. I asked John what he wanted me to specialise in. He said, 'I'd like you to prepare students especially for what may come from left field. So many people today, young and old alike, fall apart when trauma and tragedy strike. They need a lot of help with ways to cope. Be yourself and tell stories. Tell everyone where you've come from and how you got here.' A formal job description was written for me later, but John's proved to be quite prophetic and profound. He really did want me to be myself and tell stories, and the importance of this was driven home to me many times during my years at the school.

John had a great gift of identifying people for roles rather than roles for people. He perceived that I was what I was, and that my past had made me. I was a grandfather figure. I was also a one-eyed person—and while on the one hand it was a disability, I didn't consider it to be a disability, and John knew it would help students to identify with me. I was also a victim of child abuse, and many students with disabilities were also. I discerningly told stories of my past, and students related to them. Stories of my parents being so poor that they didn't pay to replace my broken glass eye; of going to school with a grotesque empty eye socket and being called 'freak' and 'retard'; of having to save until I was seventeen to buy an eye.

Stories of my prison work, during which I saw many inmates with backgrounds like mine turn their lives around.

One of the most volatile students in the school said to me, 'I love the stories of your life, Bill. You know where I'm coming from. You've been there.'

Mack had just commenced at our school, and he was a very traumatised and angry adolescent. He had experienced horrific domestic abuse and had been placed in care a number of times. Staff hadn't managed to get him into a classroom yet. He would be dropped off in the foyer and immediately run down the corridors causing mayhem, smashing holes in walls, and terrorising students and staff alike.

It was decided that I would attempt to engage Mack and hopefully ease him into a classroom. He had a couple of mates at our school that he knew from outside, and I worded them up to try and convince him that I was all right and fun to hang out with. That worked, and I was able to do a couple of woodwork projects with him first thing in the morning, then take him to class. He never managed to stay there long, however, before having an altercation with someone, racing out and creating havoc again. His concentration was limited, and I could see he was getting bored with woodwork. Our school had a bakery about a ten-minute drive from the main building. Having discovered that he loved sausage rolls and was hanging out for one, I realised that this was the bait.

'Mate,' I said as he walked in next morning, 'how'd you like a freshly baked sausage roll?'

'Wow, have you got one?'

'No, but how would you like to come for a drive to get one?'

'Let's go, Bill!' he said, starting to walk out the door.

'Righto, buddy.'

For the next few days, first thing in the morning all we did was drive up to the bakery and back. He opened up increasingly as we did, and I discovered a real idiosyncrasy he had about sausage rolls. My young friend informed me that he only ate the meat and not the pastry. He hated tomato sauce as well. He insisted that the meat be carefully extracted from the pastry inside the paper bag so as to leave it intact like a shell. This was a very delicate surgical operation, but after a couple of days I became quite skilled at it.

One morning, after performing my routine sausage-roll operation, I received a flash of inspiration. Squeezing some tomato sauce on the back of my right hand, I quickly reached over, pressed it against the back of my friend's hand and said, 'We're blood brothers now, buddy!'

'Arrrh, yuck, Bill, what are you doing?'

'We're blood brothers now, mate.'

'Blood what?'

'Blood brothers.'

'What's that mean?'

'It means that when you've had the same sort of stuff happen to you, you understand each other better. Like how you've been hurt by people, and I've been hit in the eye with a knife.'

'Was it your dad who threw that knife at you, Bill?'

I realised someone must have told him that. 'No, he threw it at my mum and hit me instead. That's why I'm a one-eyed Geelong supporter!'

That went right over his head, but on the way back to school he kept saying, 'Wow! We're blood brothers.'

From that moment on Mack knuckled down in his classroom, and at the end of the year he got an award.

~

A great privilege in special education was to get to know many of the parents who care for their disabled kids. I call them 'hero parents' because that's what they are, heroes.

One of the reasons so many parents with a disabled child or children have such a hard time is that they get so little respite. Their children often have behavioural problems and idiosyncrasies. Friends and family members frequently don't know how to deal with them, so they don't deal with them and just stop visiting. Many hero parents are single mums. I once visited such a mum who had been in her new home for twelve months. 'You are the first outsider who has visited me since I shifted,' she said. That is a common scenario.

Hero parents love their children immensely and are incredibly devoted to them, often assisting them to achieve more than others thought they could. Fiercely protective and proud of their kids, these parents are proactive in advocating for them and in attempting to obtain more assistance for them and others. You will find a group of hero parents on school councils and in government bodies, the thorn in the flesh of those who want to leave radical but necessary changes in the too-hard basket.

It would be most remiss of me not to write about the amazing teaching and ancillary staff in disability education. They are heroes also, and working with them was a privilege. For the majority of them, it is a vocation. It might also be an extension of proactive parenting, because a substantial percentage of staff either have children with disabilities or have friends and relatives who do. They are quite passionate about their roles, and especially about the potential of their students. Sometimes outsiders might think that experienced staff are being harsh or cruel by insisting that students do things for themselves, but the alternative is to disrespect the capabilities of those with disabilities and to do them a disservice, as well as making a rod for parents' and carers' backs.

Visionary and entrepreneurial leaders in special education are in a special category. They are driven by a deep belief that children with disabilities need the best education and facilities possible. John is in that category. He named his school the 'specialist school' not the 'special school', and he recruited specialist staff: physiotherapists, occupational therapists, speech therapists, psychologists, and a chaplain, yours truly. Together with the school council, he provided state-of-the-art facilities second to none in the world: an educational residential unit, independent living units at the school farm, an early learning centre, two cafes and a bakery. A constant stream of students have gained hospitality training, including a number of apprentice chefs and bakers.

I well remember John going cap in hand to the state government as he endeavoured to obtain funding for the early-learning centre. He reported back at our next staff meeting that his request had been refused, adding, 'That's all right, we'll get our own funding.' And he did, via corporations again.

When I was commencing at the school, John said to me, 'I know you're not a nine-to-five man, Bill, and inevitably you'll be responding to students and parents and staff after hours, so when that is the case, compensate by arriving a little bit later.'

I said, 'I'll probably never do that, but can there be some trade-off for me to perform community roles and be a guest speaker here and there in the name of the school?' Much of that happened over the years: I was a member of the City of Ballarat Disability Advisory Committee, spoke at a national conference on TAFE education, and made presentations at many other important community seminars and meetings.

In 2007, the year after I started at the school, there was a horrific train accident near the town of Kerang in north-west Victoria. Eleven passengers were killed and twenty-three injured when a train ploughed into a truck at a level crossing. In a coronial review of the accident there was much criticism of the slow medical and pastoral response; some doctors and nurses were evidently available but not allowed to assist. Subsequently a Victorian Emergency Response Team was formed, and I was invited to join them as a chaplain and asked to be on standby with a bag packed for any major emergency.

~

During 2006 and early 2008, Bev and I had our own trials. Bev's mum had been diagnosed with dementia a number of years earlier and her condition worsened considerably through 2006. Bev's dad cared for her initially, but it became increasingly hard for him to do so, especially when Mum didn't recognise him and wouldn't allow a 'stranger' to sleep in the bed with her. It broke his heart. Bev's sister Julianne moved in to assist, but when Mum later went into a care facility, a vital part of his heart and life was torn from him. They had been married sixty-six years and were inseparable.

Dad died on the twelfth of March that same year of a broken heart. Mum hated being in the care facility and although she was not very cognisant, she was probably devastated and felt terribly alone. Mum undoubtably could not live without Dad, and died less than a month after his passing. Fortunately, Bev had been able to spend a week visiting her before she died. When her doctor informed the family that their mother had a limited time to live, I flew to Queensland as soon as I could. Though she appeared to be unconsciousness, Bev nevertheless told Mum I was on my way. My brother-in-law Bruce picked me up from the airport and took me straight to her facility. I walked up to her bedside and Bev said, 'Mum, Bill's here'. She opened her eyes, smiled and closed her eyes again. I prayed, thanking God, and she seemed very much at peace. She passed away in the early hours of the following morning. I officiated at both my father-in-law and my mother-in-law's funerals. My mother-in-law had understandably been very wary of me when Bev first introduced me to her. Then after we married I took her precious daughter to the end of the world in Melbourne and I wasn't her most popular person. But over the forty years of our marriage to that point, Mum and I had developed a real affinity for each other, especially spiritually, and we loved singing together, sometimes well into the night. Her favourite spiritual song was 'Trust and Obey'.

At the same time, my mother's health was deteriorating rapidly. She had been diagnosed with dementia some five years before and admitted into a nursing home in Eildon about three years later. Up until then her decline had been slow—in fact, from Mum's perspective it hadn't even been noticeable.

Mum still had a beautiful singing voice into her eighties. She had once visited the nursing home and performed for the residents. Then when she resided there, in her mind she was only ever visiting for a performance!

Bev and I visited Mum regularly, and towards the end of 2007 her memory had declined significantly. On one visit she appeared to be not only oblivious to our presence but also not there herself in her mind. While ignoring us, she walked over to a window, looked up and around, and asked, 'Where's Billy? Jesus, where's Billy?' Mum was already in Heaven in her mind, and she expected me to be there, which was nice and reassuring.

On the afternoon of 10 February 2008, my sister Norma rang me to say that Mum had lapsed into a coma and was not expected to see the night out. Bev and I rushed up from Buninyong and joined Norma to sit with Mum. We all spoke with her as though she was listening, believing she was. Bev and I prayed and thanked God for her, and we sang some of her favourite hymns, including 'What a Friend We Have in Jesus' and 'Blessed assurance'.

After singing 'Blessed Assurance', I was reminded of the greatest assurance of all for Mum, written by the Apostle Paul: 'Absent from the body, present with the Lord.' We were holding her hands when her spirit left her body and went to be with Jesus late that night. I officiated at Mum's funeral.

~

Bev and I had an incredibly demanding workload during 2007 while working fulltime at school and still travelling to Colac and conducting church and its programs each weekend. So as hard as it was emotionally to do so, we decided to conclude our time at the church in Colac at the end of 2007. We had invested eight years of our lives there and made many friends, both in the church and the general community.

Relieved of the need to travel to Colac and back, the pressure was taken off me considerably during 2008, but student numbers also increased significantly and with it my workload. Then suddenly in mid-August a bombshell almost as bad as my brother Gordon's death was dropped on me. Eddie had been diagnosed with very aggressive and advanced leukemia. The prognosis was so bad that he had to start treatment immediately. He was taken from his hometown in Warrnambool to Geelong's General Hospital, where he was hospitalised for an excruciating seven months until the end of March the following year. Eddie's wife Rhonda stayed with him all that time. It must have been incredibly hard for her to be confronted with Eddie's leukemia. She had battled with breast cancer herself not all that long before and was still experiencing the after-effects. Bev and I, only 80 kilometres away in Buninyong, were able to visit regularly and take a meal of Eddie's choice down every week to supplement the hospital food.

This all drove home to Bev and me how close we were to Eddie and Rhonda. Eddie had been a part of me almost all my life, and Bev had been closely involved with him also, ever since first meeting him in St George. Eddie and Rhonda married in 1971 and had three children and lived an extremely busy family, business and community service life, including much voluntary work with Rotary on overseas building projects. Despite that, we've never been out of touch, visiting and contacting one another fairly regularly. Rhonda and I have always had a close rapport, bouncing witticisms off one another and taking the micky out of each another.

It had now been been eight months since the horrific train crash at Kerang and my appointment as emergency chaplain. I was well settled into the Specialist School and having a ball. We had also settled into the Peel Street Church of Christ in Ballarat as our place of worship, where Bev became administrator and I was interim Minister and then Elder while working full-time at school. Not long after this my state emergency chaplaincy readiness was activated when a major event occurred in Victoria.

On Saturday, 7 February 2009, the devastating Black Saturday bushfires started. First thing on Monday morning I was contacted as chaplain of the state emergency response team and asked if I could head post-haste to Plenty Valley Christian College in Doreen. I was to counsel students and staff during the week.

Doreen was near the town of Kinglake, the epicentre of the horrific fires. Of the 173 tragic deaths, 120 occurred in the Kinglake area alone. There were over five hundred students at the college, and a counselling room was set up for me to assist them along with any staff members wanting support. A steady stream of upset students and staff came to see me. Some had lost friends and relatives. Several senior students were Country Fire Authority volunteers who had been swatting out burning embers, and they had witnessed horrendous scenes. You can imagine how trauma-tised they were. It was a great privilege to be there for the school throughout that very full-on week.

On the Friday afternoon I was asked to address the staff and answer questions about future strategies. I emphasised how necessary it was for them to look after their own health and well-being, and to be in 'the right space' to assist their students and one another at that crucial time. I said that ultramarathon runners have to pace themselves physically, mentally and spiritually, if they are to endure and finish the race.

After I drove back to Ballarat, I had a critical incident counselling session to debrief and off-load with a psychologist. My work with Plenty Valley Christian College was cause for much reflection, and I considered my journey over forty-five years. All along I had been repeatedly thrown into the deep end, working with vulnerable people, on the streets, in hospital, in the homes I shared with my family, in City Missions, in prisons, in church and in special education. This had been such a privilege and yet a considerable responsibility as well.

My great mentor Jack Evans had once told me, 'Bill, you've been so greatly blessed—keep passing the blessing on. It's like a relay—keep passing the baton on!' I realised how right he was. Going right back to 1964, I had been driven to pass the blessing on. More than that, I'd been called and commissioned to do so. Along the way there had been trials and tribulations, but I'd never had a job, I'd only ever had a vocation.

20

Giving thanks

Some more trials were just around the corner. In late 2011 I'd had a constricted urine flow for quite a while, then one day I was caught in a a long queue for the urinals at Melbourne Cricket Ground when someone behind me said, 'Oh, I'm so glad I had that urinary diversion procedure! My eyes aren't watering, and I don't have to cross my legs.' I laughed, and I grimaced, but more importantly when I got back to Buninyong I immediately got referred to see a urologist to undergo the same the procedure. The urologist took the opportunity to take a biopsy of my prostate for good measure. I was so confident I didn't have cancer that I didn't take Bev with me to get the results. So I was quite stunned when the urologist told me that the sample was rated seven out of ten on the Gleason scale, which meant I had quite malignant prostate cancer. My prostate needed to be removed urgently. It was the urologist's turn to be stunned when I said, 'Thank you, Lord,' an automatic and instinctive reaction. As much as I didn't feel like it, I'd proved over many years that the Bible injunction to 'give thanks in all circumstances' was incredibly helpful.

Bev was very strong and positive when I told her the news, and we decided straight away to bring our family together and let them know. And while I was also keen to inform them of my situation, I was also quite emotional. The children were very reassuring, believing—as Bev and I did—that because of early detection, the cancer was probably contained in the prostate and could hopefully be eliminated.

Something that became paramount for me was how my faith would stand up and how I would cope with the prospect of death. I had officiated at many funerals over the years and read Psalm 21 many times, part of which says, 'Though I walk through the valley of the shadow of death, I will fear no evil . . .' Now I was being put to the test, and I had no fear of death. The hereafter as well as the here were very real and assuring to me.

Having read of the increasing use and positive results of robotic surgery, I got myself referred to the Peter MacCallum Cancer Centre where it had recently become available. Mine was to be the third robotic operation in Victoria. Our daughter Pamela drove Bev and I down early on the morning of the procedure. She had booked accommodation for Bev and herself near Peter Mac, and she'd taken three days off work to wait on us hand and foot if needs be, a real godsend.

In the operating suite, I was excited as I glanced at the console that the surgeon would use to control the robot, which was covered in plastic. He had outlined the procedure: he would make five incisions in my stomach, including one in my navel. Instruments would then be placed in the incisions for the robot to use. The detached prostate would come out through my navel.

The operation went very well, although it took six and a half hours. Twenty-four hours later I returned home, days earlier than would have been the case with conventional surgery, and my recovery was excellent.

It was the last month of summer. Lying back on our lounge-room couch, I was bare-chested and wearing Geelong Football Club boxer shorts. A catheter had been inserted into my urethra and a drainage bag strapped to my right leg, with a catheter valve or tap connected to the bottom of the bag. Enter my four-year-old grandson Mitchell. Noticing tape over the holes in my stomach, he asked, 'What's that, Grandad?'

'A robot helped to fix my stomach, mate.'

'True? What for?'

'The robot cut some bad stuff out called cancer.'

Pointing to the drainage bag with a tap on the end, Mitchell asked, 'What's that for, Grandad?'

'That's the robot's cannon. I'm very sore, and if anyone tries to hurt me, the robot squirts them.'

'What does he squirt them with, Grandad?'

'Come over here, and I'll whisper it to you.' Mitchell complied, and I whispered, 'Pee.'

He giggled and then quick as a flash said, 'Call Healy, Grandad.'

Healy was our daughter's beautiful border collie. Now it was my turn to laugh—Mitchell wanted to test the robot. Healy would want to nuzzle me, nestle into me and try to put his paws on me.

Mitchell was keen to see if the robot really would protect me and shoot Healy with pee.

Just after this, Bev and I met Reg Worthy at a Prison Fellowship function. He looked old and frail, but still had the mischievous twinkle in his eye. He looked like he could still outsmart me if I tried my artificial eye in the cup of coffee trick. It was as if we had never had a falling out. I certainly felt nothing but love for him and great appreciation once more for all I'd learnt from him. Then in November 2013 we received word that Reg had passed away. Bev and I attended his memorial service. Overall it was a great tribute to a life well lived and strong testimony to extraordinary Christian and community service.

It's been said of me, 'Bill never does things in halves', and it appeared that may have been the case physically. First cancer, then just before Christmas a year later, I had a full knee replacement.

In early 2017, just before my seventy-fifth birthday, I retired from the Ballarat Specialist School. Like all the other major employment changes in my life, it proved to be a necessity. Despite how very much I had enjoyed my work, and how I missed the people immensely, in every instance there was a greater priority. In 2016 Bev had been diagnosed with vasculitis, a rare blood-vessel disease, and she had come dangerously close to being put on dialysis for both kidneys. I'd taken considerable time off school to be with her and care for her, and now there was no other thought or consideration: I must retire from school and be fully available for Bev. She had to be my main priority. I had been hers for forty-nine years of our marriage to that point.

Then, only a couple of weeks after my retirement, just after New Year's Day 2018, I learnt a lasting lesson. I was at home with

Bev as she was preparing to go to church to do the vacuuming. Although I was about to travel to Geelong to visit someone in hospital, I went with Bev to do the vacuuming as she was feeling unwell. I hadn't been vacuuming long before I started to experience pins and needles down both my arms. And then there was pain in my chest. It intensified—to the extent it felt like my chest was in a vice, being squeezed tighter and tighter. I called out to Bev, 'I'm pretty sure I'm having a heart attack. You'd better get me to hospital!'

Bad mistake. Never do this. Always call an ambulance. Ambos have all the expertise and equipment should anything go wrong.

I just about gave Bev her own heart attack as she was driving me to hospital. It was only a few blocks away, but she was encountering a conspiracy of red lights. Bev raced into casualty at St John of God Hospital in Ballarat. A team ascertained I was indeed having a heart attack, and that everything pointed to a blocked artery. I would need a stent in a hurry. However, all the theatres were closed at St John of God. Fortunately there was an overpass passage across the road to the Base Hospital, so the team rushed me over. Bev and our daughter Angela were running at a frantic pace to keep up.

Soon I was lying on the operating table as a marvellous team of cardiologists, nurses and an anaesthetist gave me a blow-by-blow description of the placing of a stent in my blocked artery. They assured me there was only one and that no damage appeared to have been done to my heart. I was actually enjoying the procedure, asking questions and then feeling the warm flow of fresh blood through the reinforced artery.

My recovery was so swift that it felt like I hadn't had a heart attack at all. I had a ball in hospital—when doctors and nurses were looking for me sometimes, I would be in other patients' rooms encouraging them and supporting them. So the moral of the story is: doing the vacuuming can be life-threatening! More importantly, had I continued to Geelong and had the heart attack enroute, I may not have survived. Divine providence? I think so.

~

Although my heart attack cut right across the purpose of my retirement for a while, it afforded me another period of reflection on my vocation—well, really it was *our* vocation. It had been a team effort always involving me, Bev and our kids. None of it would have been possible without everyone, just as I'd needed supporters during my ultramarathons.

You would have read of considerable hardships along the way for Bev and our seven children. Yet our kids will tell you that it was the making of them: not being born with silver spoons in their mouths, not having everything at their fingertips, having to think for themselves and be resourceful—and, perhaps most importantly, being surrounded by needy people while learning to identify with and care for them.

Two of our daughters, Angela and Sara, are in the welfare field. Angela has worked for many years in juvenile justice, refugee aid and residential care, and she currently manages the welfare services for an Indigenous community in the Northern Territory. Sara has worked in nursing and is the owner and CEO of a disability service provider; she works with many of my former students.

Pamela has been a leading secretary and manager in local councils and at universities for many years. Currently she's Advancement Manager (Global and Engagement) for Federation University. She is one of the Future Shapers on the Committee for Ballarat and an advocate for the homeless.

Christine majored in journalism at university but preferred advertising and worked with the Launceston *Examiner* and the Brisbane *Courier-Mail* newspapers in that field. She owned an advertising technology business in Malaysia for over twenty years and has constantly encouraged other women into business and mentored them there.

Our sons are in engineering. David is in mechanical engineering, having managed plants in Australia, New Zealand and South-East Asia. Paul is a joint proprietor of his own engineering business, and Mark is an international IT architect.

~

All our resilience has been put to the test while we've been living through the Covid pandemic that commenced in March 2020. One of the worst aspects for a close family like ours was not being able to see our overseas children and grandchildren for over twelve months. Even those living nearby were locked down periodically and unable to embrace one another.

Hospital visits weren't allowed in Victoria for over two years, and that put us to the greatest test of all on 21 January 2022. Bev had a major heart attack and needed to have a stent inserted. During the procedure it was revealed that she needed two more stents, but she was too unwell for them to be inserted then. She was sent home and returned in two weeks for the other stents. While the medical team were operating, she had another heart attack.

Throughout almost a month of tsunami emotions, no hospital visits were allowed. Hovering overhead was the dark cloud of real-isation that the only exception would be if Bev were to become terminally ill. 'Love never fails', however, and ingenuity made a way for us to have a special whole-family visit. One Saturday morning I arranged for as many family members as possible to meet under Bev's second-floor hospital window. Some thirty of us assembled with balloons and 'We love you, Gma' banners. Bev was deeply moved, and it was some compensation for all of us to visit in this virtual way.

I keep telling Bev that she's fortunate that she's got a young man in her life to assist her—me! She replies with some words of Solomon from the Bible: 'Vanity of vanities, all is vanity'! Quite seriously, though, someone asked me recently, 'Bill, how are you travelling?' I answered: 'Well, despite having had prostate cancer and a heart attack that required a stent, and many carcinomas removed and a full knee replacement in recent years, I really am very fit and healthy. I've been so fortunate. One carcinoma was quite large and deep in my left eye socket. The only problem is that after surgery to remove it, my prized prosthetic 'Geelong' eye no longer fits! (I had promised myself that if Geelong won the 2007 AFL Grand Final, I would get a Geelong prosthetic eyeball made, logo and all. They did win and I kept my word. Maybe I'm the only genuine one-eyed Geelong supporter.) One of my Bible heroes, Caleb, said at age eighty-five, 'I'm as strong today as I was at forty; give me this mountain'. In my eightieth year, that's how I feel. I'm planning to walk/run 80 kilometres on my eightieth birthday next April. I'm so grateful to my surgeon and staff at the Ballarat Skin Cancer Centre. They give me a periodical all-over body check and have literally saved my life.

Epilogue

Ever since my conversion, I have been driven to give my absolute hundred per cent to whatever I put my hands to. Early on in my journey, a number of Bible verses spelt this out for me. One was, 'Whatever your hands find to do, do it with all your might.' Another was, 'Study to show yourselves approved by God, workers that need not be ashamed.'

I have indeed been driven. Driven to give those from my background the same dreams and visions and inspiration for a bright future that I was given. Driven to prove people wrong who think that some people can't achieve great things. Driven to be the same encourager and mentor that others have been to me. Driven to be a good role model and hopefully an example of how 'bad stuff' in our lives can be overcome by replacing it with 'good stuff'. Above all, absolutely driven to prove that there are no greater powers or miracles on earth than the power of Divine love and the power of forgiveness.

Having read *Driven*, my hope and prayer is that you might be driven also. That you might realise your destiny on Earth of leaving a positive mark. Not just in concrete at Hollywood, but in people's lives. May people be so thankful that you lived because they now really live. Get on with it and God bless.

Bill Sutcliffe

Acknowledgements

Putting this book together has been a mammoth effort. Firstly I'm very appreciative of my publisher, Allen & Unwin, for giving this first-time author a go. Their publishing director Tom Gilliatt, publisher Annette Barlow and freelance editor Kate Goldsworthy have been terrific with their assistance and encouragement, as has Samantha Kent, the in-house editor who project-managed *Driven* beautifully through to the printing stage.

The documentary maker Andrew Parisi and his journalist partner Simone have been so very generous in giving me liberal advice and vital contacts. John Burt OAM graciously wrote the foreword.

Above all, thanks to my family, who have assisted in whatever ways they could when I was writing and still working fulltime, and ever since. Our daughter Pamela, in particular, has done an incredible job of typing and retyping copious copies of my scribbled writings, voice recordings and subsequent computer drafts. I am very indebted to each of you. 'Thank you' is far from enough. I hope you will be richly rewarded by the knowledge that you have assisted many people to receive help and hope through this book.

Driven is an acknowledgement of the vital roles that mentors and other inspirational people have played in my life. Some of them were literally life-savers to me, and I owe a great debt to them, in particular Eileen Burgess, Mr McQuirter, Powder-Monkey Jimmy, Senior Constable Frank Mannix, Mr Godfrey, Charlie and Des Wood, Stan Fletcher, Jack and Ollie Evans, and the youth group in St George, and especially Desley and Max Fletcher.

It goes without saying that my wife Bev has been a greater part of my life and more influential than anyone else, other than God. She was instrumental in my becoming a Christian, and we have been married fifty-five years. Bev could have had any career she chose, but she sacrificed her personal prospects to serve God and work with me. Despite that she has held offices of secretary, treasurer, manager, administrator, Sunday school teacher, youth leader, and religious education teacher in schools for over thirty years. Bev is a brilliant storyteller and has kept listeners enthralled in churches, Sunday schools and public schools for many years. She has also achieved a Diploma of Publishing (Professional Book Editing, Proofreading, and Publishing) through the Australian College QED. To say that I am indebted to her and in awe of her is an understatement.